Flasher

A Memoir

Unbearable Books from Autonomedia

Series Editors: Jim Feast and Ron Kolm

UB—1: *Spermatagonia: The Isle of Man,* bart plantenga
UB—2: *Negativeland,* Doug Nufer
UB—3: *Neo Phobe,* Jim Feast with Ron Kolm
UB—4: *Shorts Are Wrong,* Mike Topp
UB—5: *The Hotel of Irrevocable Acts,* Carl Watson
UB—6: *The Ass's Tale,* John Farris
UB—7: *This Young Girl Passing,* Donald Breckenridge
UB—8: *Love Does Not Make Me Gentle or Kind,* Chavisa Woods
UB—9: *A Superintendent's Eyes,* Steve Dalachinsky
UB—10: *Kali's Day,* Bonny Finberg
UB—11: *The Rat Hunt Boys,* Anna Mockler
UB—12: *The Beer Mystic,* bart plantenga
UB—13: *Night Shift,* Ron Kolm
UB — 14: *Pareidolia,* Carl Watson
UB — 15: *Long Day, Counting Tomorrow,* Jim Feast with Carol Wierzbicki
UB — 16: *Flasher,* Tsaurah Litzky
UB — 17: *Welcome Distractions,* Carol Wierzbicki

Flasher

A Memoir

Tsaurah Litzky

Autonomedia

Acknowledgements

I am ever grateful to Ron Kolm, Jim Feast, Jim Fleming and Unbearables/Autonomedia for making *Flasher: A Memoir* into a print book. This was my dream and their vision, good counsel and hard work made it real.

Many kudos to Danny Shot for his invaluable support, great help in shepherding the book into being and to Julia Faye Litzky for her invaluable support and technical acumen. Thanks to Carol Wierzbicki for her editing chops and encouragement. Thanks to Ethan Cornell for his encouragement and computer expertise.Thanks to Davidson Garrett for the About the Author photo.

Thanks to the now defunct *Arts Weekly, Downtown,* where I worked as a columnist from 1993 to 1997. Some of those columns over time morphed into parts of this book.

My gratitude to Long Shot Press which published *Flasher: A Memoir* as an e-book for Kindle in 2013 and to Audible Books which published it 2013. Thank you Susie Bright for making this possible and thank you so much for your support and encouragment.

Thank you to my dentist Paul Teplitsky, for keeping me smiling.

ISBN: 978-1-57027-334-6

Unbearable Books are published and distributed by

Autonomedia
POB 568 Williamsburgh Station
Brooklyn NY 11211-0568 USA

www.autonomedia.org
info@autonomedia.org

Contents

Flasher

A Memoir

Dedication

Flasher is dedicated to my family, my mother Ruth, father Jerry, brother Joel, niece Julia and nephew Matt.

It's dedicated to those who were happy to have me use their real names as well as those I knew better than to even ask.

This is for my Friends of the Heart, (you know who you are).

This is for Virgos, slow dancing, gelato, avocados, Eros, libidos and pouring another glass.

This is for the clean brush, the royal flush, transcendence, astonishment, pursuing excellence, breaking chains, and the hush that comes before the darkness catches flame.

Author's Prologue

Flasher: A Memoir is the story of a certain ten years in my life: 1988–1998. It is the story of the different lives I lived within that time. Sometimes I was a baby, naive as a new blade of grass. Other times I thought I knew everything, even enough to control my own destiny; what a great big, blooming ass I was.

Flasher: A Memoir is about negotiating transits, how it happens as the seasons go by (although sometimes it can happen in a second), you find yourself in circumstances you could never have imagined. I would ask myself how, why did this or that happen to me? Was it fate, luck, chance, a combination of the three? Some days I would tend to believe the "why" was explained by synchronicity and the theories of causal connection set forth by C.G. Jung. Other days I believed it was in the power of Yoga.

This book is about how I became a prodigal daughter, a *femme fatale* — expert at falling in and out of love, a writer, a poet, a wife, a wanderer, a better friend, and a quick-change artist.

While the action does briefly move to Amsterdam and also to Provincetown and back, *Flasher: A Memoir* is mostly set in New York City, the Lower East Side and Brooklyn. It encapsulates a fertile and fevered segment of the then flourishing New York arts scene. G.W. Bush and Bill Clinton were the presidents. It describes the times before 9/11, before cell phone mania, arguably simpler times?

At a New Year's day night party in Williamsburg, I meet a sculptor who works in leather and designs fetish wear and sex chairs. The book then becomes a consideration of the possibilities of True Love and of Sexual Freedom, if there is such a thing? *Flasher: A Memoir* considers the value of friendship and families; real families and the families we assemble around ourselves. These are familiar questions.

It is not my intention to provide answers. The libraries are crowded with books attempting to explain this "stuff." Instead, I sincerely hope you enjoy the story of this pilgrim's progress through the irregular fields of love. Maybe you will have a few laughs at my mistakes, whether they resemble any of yours or not. Without laughter there is no fun, joy or saving grace? Maybe you will even be encouraged to write your own memoir? Who knows?

Tsaurah Litzky

My Own Personal Twelve-Step Program

It will take more than twelve steps for me to climb out of this hole I'm in, maybe I should dig a few feet deeper and I'll hit China, but I can't eat with chopsticks, the clothes there won't fit over my hips and I don't speak the language, but then I don't speak the language much here either. No one calls me up except an occasional three-a.m.-wrong number and this fascinating I.V. drug user who wants to be my lover. He is penniless, living in the park, but manages to scrounge up the change to call me almost daily. It is terribly depressing to me that he has the best sense of humor of any man I've ever met, and the one time I let him kiss me I had to tear myself away and run into the nearest bodega or I would have lost my soul, sorry chameleon that it is.

Only the bodega was not a bodega, but one of those drug stores where you buy minute bags of grass and four-day-old copies of *El Diario*. There were no groceries in sight except for a box of Scooter Pies that was either half empty or half full, depending on whether you hold a Manichean or Aristotelian view of the universe. Still, I asked for a packet of Kleenex because I wanted to wipe my lipstick-smeared, garish face; of course, the man behind the counter said they didn't have any Kleenex, but he gave me some toilet paper. I cleaned my face and bought a couple of Scooter Pies and, when I stepped out of the Bodega, my junkie friend was gone. He called me that night and pretended the whole incident had never happened. He told me he was buying me a diamond, he had already ordered it, three carats, marquise cut. He is so charming, he calls me Esmeralda, says I'm the world's most perfect gem.

I tried to stop wanting him. I went to the Baths on Tenth Street, poured gallons of icy water on my head. I brought home a twenty-four-year-old actor with thighs like pistons who smoked all my grass and made rugby love that left me with bruised knees, bruised elbows, bitten nipples and purple marks on my neck. When I saw the purple marks I remembered how my I.V.-using-would-be lover told me he never shot up, he was only into blow. Did I want to see his arms? When I asked, "What are those scabs on your neck?" he said, "Oh, I cut myself shaving."

I heard they have these Twelve Step programs for the families and lovers of addicts. They call these co-dependent groups or something, but I don't need to go to one of these groups; I already know I am a patsy. I don't need to sit in a smoky room and drink bad coffee to know an addict will lie as easily as piss or breathe. I already know because Rudy stole my money and magic chicken-bone necklace twenty years ago, because my father told us the family car got wrecked when his bookie re-possessed it, because I blew the rent on a suede coat that was supposed to restore my vanished hippie beauty and then told the landlord I was mugged.

I know because I steal to the refrigerator late at night and eat all the chili I made to last a week in one terrible gulp and then I call my friend Jan, first thing in the morning, and say I'm starved, I haven't eaten for two days, please take me to breakfast at Vaselka's. It will take more than 12,000 steps for me to surrender my compulsions, my shopping binges, my orgies of masturbation, my paranoia.

I think no one likes me. I'm not getting invited to parties, other women hate me because they suspect my secret; I'm not a woman at all, but a gray rain cloud with an androgynous mind and a ravenous catfish, a bottom feeder, for a sex. It didn't help last week when my friend C. told me that Z., another poet, was dissing me everywhere behind my back. I was shocked. Isn't she in one of those Twelve Step programs where they teach compassion, where they teach love thy neighbor, the wretched, the fearful, the lonely; or maybe that's some other program, Christianity or folk dancing or word perfect?

My own Twelve Step program is yet to be written and if I ever climb out of this abyss of self-loathing and learn to believe in myself, I'll write you a letter. I'll tell you how I did it, I'll let you know.

Fallout Follies

I'm floating belly-up like a dead rat in the sewer of what was once my self-respect. My obsessions make me ashamed, abject, and hopeless. Like everlasting halitosis or a perpetual boner under the raincoat, my obsessions render me unfit for the companionship of friends.

I can't stop saying "Thank you" when I receive a gift or compliment. I can't stop using words I hate like karma, relationship and love. I go back up four flights of stairs three times to see if I have locked my apartment door. When I see a man with a beard I always break out in a sweat, even though I use two kinds of deodorant, Ban and Ice Blue Secret. When the temperature goes above ninety degrees, as it has for the last four days, I add a third deodorant, Mennen's Extra Strength. I only eat the crusts of bread; I never eat eggs because they are embryos. I hallucinate horrors. This week will be the forty-eighth anniversary of the bombings of Hiroshima and Nagasaki, so I am seeing mushroom clouds everywhere: outside my kitchen window, in the sky above the bank on Houston Street, exploding from the ears of my waitress at Sidewalk. I tip her too much because I don't want her to know I'm crazy, that I'm hallucinating, that I'm inadequate and petty as a pincushion. I am a pincushion — my hallucinations are the pins.

Because I'm obsessed, I leave Sidewalk and go out into the muggy summer night. I walk through Tomkins Square Park and I see my I.V.-using-would-be-lover who is now homeless and keeping company with a gaggle of teenage runaways who hang out in the park. He's got a fifteen-year-old boy with the face of an angel trotting after him like a dog. He tells me he is protecting the poor kids from chicken hawks. He says he offers guidance, hands out condoms. When I ask if he really thinks I'm gonna believe that crap, he says when I get angry my eyes sparkle like fireflies. He wants me to believe he is the Johnny Appleseed of Ramses, the Robin Hood of Fourex, but when I look at him I see a canceled check, a human wreck with an infected ear.

Drops of pus trail down his neck next to the string of tracks that hang there like Mardi-Gras beads. Why do I want to put my head on his chest and hold him?

I have read in David McCullough's biography of Truman that at Hiroshima people vanished completely into the air, they vaporized or burned to a cinder standing up. Women whose skin hung from them like kimonos ran shrieking into the rivers. How dare I even talk about pain and glorify my juvenile complaints? Maybe that's my karma, to be consumed by banal concerns, futile follies, just as it is the karma of my I.V.-using-would-be-lover to be a compulsive, lying charmer, hitting on every soul he meets for a dollar, a quarter, or pretty please, one tiny dime. It was Truman's karma to decide to drop that bomb. He complained of terrible headaches afterwards.

"Physical or figurative?" they asked.

"Both," he replied.

In time he got over the headaches and went on to play the piano at White House dinners.

I know my collection of tacky, erotic lingerie, my many fantasies of spanking, bondage and humiliation connect me to what is considered most abhorrent, and thereby to me the most radical and fascinating, in American culture. I look around the park and everywhere I see bare arms, legs, necks, covered with geometric tribal tattoos. I see pierced nipples, navels, eyebrows. People are turning themselves into pincushions, and in a very public way; maybe I'm not so alone in my obsessions.

A book of Neal Cassidy's prison writing has been published under the title *Grace Beats Karma*. This is one book I will never read. No way I will do anything to detract from the exquisite promise of that title. If grace beats karma, there is still a remote chance for me, if only I can overcome my narcissism long enough to take a stand.

I am invited to read at a coffee shop where the owner promises to split the take at the door with the three poets reading. He makes at least fifty bucks, than says he says he can't give us any money because he didn't make enough. I decide to confront him.

"You said you'd split with us," I say. "You didn't even give us a cup of coffee." I get excited, lose control, my hands whip through the air.

"Don't point your finger at me," he says. What would he prefer, an Uzi, a big black dildo, a kazoo? Doesn't he know that, without poetry, music, art, the world would be a puddle of piss? Of course, I am licked, trapped in the timeless confrontation between the artist and the philistine, the one in which the philistine gets fatter and fatter and the artist gets more and more suicidal. His partner chimes in and says, "We let you poets read here and you don't even spend two bucks."

Maybe I'll let him suck my new tribal tattoo if I ever have the courage to get one. Maybe I don't need a tattoo, my twisted karma wraps around my legs like barbed wire pulling me down into the void. Maybe it's my karma, my fate, my folly to keep beating my head against the wall, but it's better than no karma at all. I have to believe, in order to go on, if all the writers, artists, painters and musicians in America jammed into the Starship Enterprise and took off to chronicle the unknown galaxies of space, we would be missed. A black ash of desolation would spread out over this pitiful country and bury it under an enormous mushroom cloud.

Daddy

My father needed a hernia operation. His doctor told him if he didn't do it right away, his gonads would fall to the floor. My brother, who had been on duty when my father got a plastic heart valve last year, called from Maryland and told me it was my turn. I couldn't argue.

Riding down on the Amtrak in my twenty-dollar, thrift-store black leather coat, I felt as elegant as Mata Hari, yet as I made my way to the dining car, none of the men working at their laptops looked up. A conductor gave me a wink, but men in uniform do nothing for me. The correlation between my proclivity to fantasize and my inability to connect with a man is one I have spent years trying to understand. It may have something to do with the way I pulled my pants down in the schoolyard to let the boys see my privates, or it may have something to do with the way my mother ran the show. I could never do anything right; if I washed a dish, she washed it over again. She always called my father Daddy, but he wasn't much of a Daddy. He hid behind his newspapers and never interfered with how she was raising us. He didn't pay any attention, to me, showed no interest in the poems I started to write when I was nine years old. Whenever I approached him to show him one, he'd say, "Go, away, I'm thinking about something." He took a second job in the evenings. He gambled, ran around. We barely saw him.

I like to think I am over my anger with my parents, that I am too busy living my life; at least they got me here. I tell myself they didn't mean to hurt me and my brother, didn't know what they were doing. Who does?

"So how's my daughter?" was the first thing my father said when he met me at the train station. In the car he told me how worried he was because his two-month-old grandson, Matthew, courtesy of my brother and his wife, has such a pointed head. "How's my daughter?" he asks again. "Are you happy?"

After we were in bed at night, my brother and I would hear our parents fighting. We thought it was about money, but later we found out my father had a mistress named Hortense. Now my father seems to blame himself because I'm living a life he can't understand.

"Keeping busy?" he asks. "Enjoying yourself? What do you do at night, where do you go?" he wants to know. "If you need money, don't be shy," he says. He wants me to exonerate him, hasn't caught on that he has to make his own peace with how he treated us. Maybe he hopes if I tell him I fly around to garden parties in helicopters and dance till dawn with famous sports personalities, the pains in his chest will go away and he can get good night's sleep.

"Sure I'm happy," I say.

As soon as I get in the door my mother starts to give me the things she has been saving for me: a bottle of real Fragonard perfume that her sister, my Aunt Mildred, brought back from Paris; a paper bag full of penny rolls; a red rubber circle the size of a pot holder to help me take stubborn lids off jars.

Can this tiny old lady in Nikes be the same woman who once said to me "Don't let a man put that thing in you until you have the ring on your finger because to a man, one hole is the same as another in the dark." I show my parents an article on Beat sexism I have written. My mother says she is too nervous about my father's surgery tomorrow to read anything; then she goes into the next room to iron his underwear as she has been doing for fifty-one years. My father reads it; my vocabulary is beautiful, he says, but the ideas are way over his head.

When my brother telephones to ask, "Have they driven you crazy yet?" I laugh, ha-ha. He tells me a hernia operation is a common outpatient procedure; we should be in the hospital five hours max.

The next morning we take a taxi so we don't have to worry about parking. When we get there, my mother takes money from her purse and hands it to my father so he can pay the cabdriver. In the waiting room, my mother excuses herself to go the ladies' room. A hospital volunteer in a pink outfit comes over to greet my father and me. She checks his name against a list she is carrying on a clipboard, and then says to him brightly, "With such a pretty young wife, I know you'll get well real fast."

When my mother returns from the ladies room, we don't tell her what the aide said. The anesthesiologist comes to get my father, and my parents embrace so ardently that for just a moment I can see them as young lovers.

My mother and I don't have much to say to each other while we are waiting; we read. A surgeon comes out in scrubs and tells the two women next to us that the good news is that the growth he removed from their mother's colon does not appear to be cancerous. "Of course," he adds, "we have to wait a couple of days for the tests to be sure. The bad news," he says, "is that the growth was so large we had to remove half her colon and her spleen. Don't worry," he adds. "Half a colon is enough."

After we hear this my mother and I can't concentrate on our books. "Why hasn't our surgeon been out to talk to us?" my mother asks. "It's been two hours. What's taking so long?" She begins pacing the waiting room. I tell her to stay calm and not to get agitated, then I dash to the cafeteria and down three cheese danishes. When I return, my mother is still pacing. Finally, our surgeon comes out and tells us everything is okay. The operation took so long because the hernia was so big. My father is in recovery and wants the newspaper so he can read the sports page. When we go in to see him, he smiles up weakly. "How's my daughter?" he asks.

Back at the house, my father vanishes into their bedroom. My mother goes into the kitchen to make him an ice pack; he calls out my name. I rush in. He is standing with his pants dropped to his ankles.

"Look," he says, pointing to a small, vertical bandage just above his crotch."That's where they went in. They had to make so many stitches. Why did I wait so long?" He shakes his head. "I can never do anything right." His belly and pubes are shaved and his penis looks white and innocent, small as a boy's. His eyes are very wide. I realize he is stoned out of his gourd on painkillers and is showing me his wound the way a child would show off a cut or scratch. He shows no embarrassment about revealing his scrawny thighs, his nakedness. After all, am I not his child, the fruit of his loins, the flesh of his flesh?

Terrorists

There are terrorists everywhere. They hide inside the black lycra tights I wear because I think they make my legs look thin. They sit inside the red enamel box that holds my stale stash of condoms, they're making the horns behind my head when I look in the mirror. A terrorist just called on the telephone impersonating my mother.

"Daddy feels you don't visit us enough," she said. "We're not getting any younger, you know? Why can't you come and visit us more often?" There are terrorists in this third cup of coffee, terrorists that may push me out into the street and force me to climb the cables of the Brooklyn Bridge screaming enough, enough, enough! My neighbor, Mary, thinks that the Arab guys that run the taxi and limousine service downstairs are terrorists. They spend half their time tinkering beneath the hoods of their cars and the rest of the time watching TV in the back of the store. They don't speak English, they wear pointy shoes and their taxis never seem to go out on calls. I don't care. I am too busy trying to co-exist with the terrorists that live between my ears. Once, I went to bed with an Arab guy who told me he could come five times in a night. He lied, he lied big time. In the morning he pulled a thick gold ring out of his pocket and put it on the fourth finger of his left hand. "Look what I have," he said, and now the terrorists have planted a married man right in the middle of his life.

When we look at each other; the air between us crackles and pops. He tells me his wife is a wonderful person, but they have been together for ten years and the magic is gone. He says I'm stunning and that I make him feel like a teenager with his first crush. I meet his wife at the health club and am surprised at how pretty and nice she is. The next time I see him at the bar I tell him that an affair is out of the question, that his wife seems very lovely and that I'm not one to muck around in other people's lives. He tells me that we are artists, that we don't live in a world of categories. He says it is no accident that he and I have met and that no one belongs to anyone else. I agree with him about the "no one belongs to anyone else part." Then, I think about how a woman who does it with a married man is considered a harlot, a housewrecker, but a man who does it with a married woman is considered to be doing her a favor. Before my married suitor leaves the bar he gives me a light kiss on the mouth and whispers, "please, please."

I have only once knowingly gone to bed with a married man. My best friend Sheilah's husband had been after me for three years. He dropped in once when I was very down in the dumps. He promised she would never know. He pounded away so hard on top of me I thought he would break me in two. Every thrust sent stronger waves of nausea, guilt and shame through me. I had betrayed my best friend for a lousy fuck. After they were divorced she told me he confessed he had seduced all of her friends, but I was the one who had resisted the longest. I did not feel redeemed.

Could I be even more desperate now than I was then? Could I ever be content sweeping the crumbs from another woman's table? I find myself lying in bed, thinking about my married suitor. He's stocky, has a strong back, solid haunches, a stallion. I wonder if he would let me spank him. He comes into the bar with a book of my poems he has bought. I inscribe it "Why not?" and add my phone number.

The next day I come home from work and find a letter from my landlord saying he had information saying I have built an illegal loft bed and that I must tear it out immediately. The terrorist impersonating my mother calls and tells me my father's hernia operation wasn't successful and has to be done over again. Can I come down like I did last month for the first operation and help them through it? I go up to the video store to get a tape, a movie to cheer me up, Dazed and Confused, but when I get back I am so despondent that I don't even have the will to put it in the VCR. I am eating a pint of double chocolate frozen yogurt when the phone rings. I pick it up and a female voice I don't recognize says, "I don't like what you wrote, you ugly bitch. Your breasts hang down like pancakes and I may just flatten them. You have a face like a dog." I was horrified into silence. Could this be some lunatic who was offended by something I wrote in one of my articles for Downtown, and how did the lunatic get my unlisted phone number? The disembodied voice floated like an oil slick out into my room.

"Stay away from my man, stay away from my man, stay away from my man, you ugly slut or I'll kick in your face," she sang to the tune of "Happy Birthday." Then she slammed the receiver down. I recognized the voice of the pretty woman whom I had met in the health club, the wife. She had gotten hold of the book I had signed for the husband. Is this woman a total nut case, or had she seen Fatal Attraction one time too many? Is the husband a womanizer? Does he get off on women fighting over him? Did he set this up? I toy with going against my principles and screwing a married man. Then the terrorists blow me away. I tell myself I'm lucky that I didn't do it with him, and this was a warning. I got off easy, but I am badly shaken.

It is no picnic living in a world that still forces so many women to find their validity through identification with a man. At least, I have my typewriter. It does not keep me warm in bed at night, but it is the only weapon I know how to use to flush out terrorists, expose them and beat them at their own game.

Birthday Girl

I'm fifty years old today and I still get weak in the knees when I experience desire. I'm fifty years old and I'm still picking my nose, eating the icing off the cake, hugging myself to sleep. I make faces in the mirror, pretending to be Greta Garbo, who shares my birthday, only I don't want to be alone but I would rather be alone than strung out, blown out or turned inside out trying to make someone love me. I will not share a meal, let alone prepare a meal, or have sex, with anyone who puts me down. I won't tolerate a disparaging comment about one of my friends and I would rather use a dildo than share my bed with a man who lies to me.

I'm fifty years old and I stopped counting my lovers after I reached a hundred. Sometimes I pass one of my old one-night stands on the street and we don't say hello. I'm sure this has nothing to do with me being fifty years old; usually I've forgotten his name and I bet he has either forgotten mine or wishes he had forgotten it.

I have never sold it, never taken money for love, but once when my toilet overflowed on Christmas Eve, the only emergency plumber my landlord could find was this Jewish guy from Borough Park who looked like Kirk Douglas in "Spartacus."I offered the plumber tequila and grass, told him it was important to be open to new experiences and seduced him. In the middle of the act, he murmured with some surprise, "She likes it, she likes it, she likes it."

Who knows what he was used to?

The next morning I found fifty dollars under my pillow, which I spent on more grass.

When I was eleven I read in Lady Chatterley's Lover that a woman has to live her life, or else regret not having lived it. This had a profound effect on me, and I resolved to become an adventuress and fly all over the world. Since then I have had many, many adventures, but most of the flying I have done has been in my head. I have been in love four times when my love has been reciprocated fully. There is nothing finer than the harmony of souls when your bodies move effortlessly together and everything fits. I have been fortunate enough to know the magnificent pleasure of bringing a lover coffee in the morning and knowing exactly every way, every place his body has been marked.

I have lived long enough to hear of the deaths of several of my lovers. Willy loved to make love with me when I had my period. He called it the spice time. He and Stevie from Max's went down to Mexico to do a grass deal. When he didn't come back for two months, Galahad called his mother. She told him Willy had been shot to death in Cuernavaca. Peter Murphy died of pneumonia just after he became famous as an underground cartoonist. Dickie O., my Provincetown fisherman is the one I think about the most. Our song was Octopus Garden. He had a bristly moustache like a catfish. He could make me come by just rubbing it across my clit. When his boat went down, of the eight men aboard, he was the one whose body was never found.

I have had some rough times: I have been raped twice, had four abortions and one miscarriage. I have disappointed some people who loved me and abandoned friends because their desperation reminded me of my own. My I.V.-using-would-be lover just abandoned me. He no longer calls me because I have refused his pleas to come live with me until he finds something more permanent. He says my new haircut looks butch and that I will die alone. I have found great consolation in friendship, and if Galahad hadn't caught me when, stoned, I stepped backwards down the ladder of the fire escape, I might now be dead. I am very grateful for my other wonderful friends, to name just a few, Laurie, Art and Jossy, Margo, Nathan. I miss my old friends, the ones with whom I have lost touch, and wonder where they are now, especially Judy Malone. We used to pick up young male hitchhikers in her car when we were driving around on the cape. We took them to the pinewoods behind Herring Cove and had our way with them.

Once, in Provincetown, on the day of Blessing Of The Fleet, when I walked past the Surf Club in my yellow bikini, thirty drunken fishermen ran out on the street and cheered. I was, and still am, very vain. I miss-used my beauty, traded on it, flaunted it, condescended to women who were not so blessed. Now that I'm fifty years old I'm learning my lesson. I'm learning what it is like to sit all night in the bar while the younger, prettier women are getting the rush, and I know it serves me right for putting too much value on superficial things. One day my body will be a shell and my face a wrinkled mask, but I hope that by then my spirit will be so light, I will not need this wretched rack of bone to carry it.

Flies

There are flies in my apartment, even though it's November. They are so bold, they buzz around my shoulders as I sit at my typewriter. I wonder if they are my dead lovers, come back to distract me from writing stories about them. They circle around my head, a few daring kamikaze flies peck at my nose. Their mouthparts suck and hiss; you have had your fun already, why make us ridiculous, let us rest. I tell them to go away. I own my life and, while I have it, everything in it is mine to examine. There is no tiny bruise or faded fingerprint that will not be analyzed if it might yield even a moment's respite from the nagging suspicion that it's already too late, that I've wasted too much time.

There is a man who wants me. He is forty-five, clean-shaven, gainfully employed. He brought me an Italian dinner and I let him kiss me, but as I told my friend Dave, it was hard work, a chore, accepting his kiss. I wanted it to be over.

"You can teach him how to kiss," Dave said.

"I am not going to teach a forty-five year old man how to kiss," I replied. Actually his kiss was proficient, subtly exploring, a little suction, just a hint of tongue, but it was that what I sensed inside the kiss was something moist and spongy, a vacuum pulling me down.

A mutual friend introduced us. During our dinner, I asked why he had wanted to meet me. He said because I am small, he likes small women, and because I seemed nice. If only he had said because you are the wild, wild wind and a satin sprouting flower. I think maybe I could go to bed with him for comfort, for simple pleasure, but then I realize that that is absurd. I am too far-gone to take anything lightly and, for me, simple pleasure is a contradiction in terms, a mythical beast, a chimera with the head of a lion, the body of a goat, and a snake for a tail.

More than once, that snake has coiled around my ankle and pulled me down into the bog, the quicksand. Every time, so far I have escaped at the last minute, my desperate will to live propelling me out of the mire towards the shore. I crawled away spluttering, shattered, my pride diminished, but still breathing, still alive. The last time Bobby B. was inside me on the daybed in my brother's recreation room in Crownsville, Maryland, I felt the earth shake just like in a tacky romance novel. The next day, when he got into his old Corvette and drove south, I knew I would never see him again. He had taken eighty dollars out of my wallet. He was a bounder, a user, a liar and a cheat. He two-timed me with a nurse from New Jersey and with a woman who worked in a copy shop, but when he was inside me I felt so connected to the music of the universe that I was at peace.

Last night I dreamed that I was in bed with a man whose face I could not see. We made love, and then he rolled over and away, turning his back to me like a blank page. I put my hand on his shoulder, tried to embrace him and curl around him, spoon-fashion, but he shrugged my hand off, pulled away, then curved further into himself. In the dream this happened again and again. When I woke up the sheets were damp and smelled of sex; but there was no man in the bed. My only companions were the flies. I could not fall back to sleep and I remembered how, at my birthday party last month, an old swain and his girlfriend gave me a huge, black coffee cup that said, in red letters, "It's the Big 50." I thanked them graciously and the next day threw the cup in the garbage. If the cup had flowers, or even kittens, on it I might have kept it.

Even though I always say that there is only the now, I realize that, since my birthday, I have been worried about the future and where I will be in twenty years. I refuse to give up on the possibilities of love. I pluck the hair from around my nipples, give myself bikini waxes, shave my legs and oil my body, all the while I am doing this I know it is more than physical love that I want. I also know that all the love in the world cannot save me but if I had a man in my bed it might be easier to sleep. As it is, I get up and go into the bathroom and get the Nyquil bottle off the shelf where it sits next to my ginseng anti-aging cream. Though I never get colds, I go through three bottles of Nyquil a month. I tell myself I am not an addict because if I was, I would carry the bottle with me at all times. I down two shots and soon I am floating in Nyquil never-never land. When the phone rings, the clock says it is

6 a.m. It is my I.V.-drug-using would-be lover whom I have not heard from in two months. He is calling to tell me he has good news. His AIDS test is negative, and he will be over in twenty minutes, no, make it half an hour. I tell him he needs two AIDS tests to be sure and that I will not even let him in the door until he is clean and has been going to N.A. for at least a year. He says I'm cutting off my nose to spite my face. He is a prize; I should grab him; I'm the kind of woman who is never satisfied.

Maybe he is right, but I am proud of my inability to compromise. It keeps me going, and when or if I grow too weak to take care of myself, I'll drink twenty bottles of blue-green Nyquil and let the flies carry me to Paradise.

My Gun

The picture of the twenty-five-caliber, six-shot, Phoenix Arms Raven I saw on the cover of *Newsday* reminds me of the little silver mace gun I bought from Earl, the bouncer at Max's, twenty-five years ago. When I would put the little silver gun in my pocket and go out late at night on the prowl, I felt like Wonder Woman. I am prone to delusions of grandeur, maybe because I am four feet, eleven inches tall, and although it shot mace, not bullets, I thought that the little gun, plus my natural intelligence would make me the physical equal of any man.

One night, after Dennis had invited me to a party in Park Slope, I dropped the little gun into the pocket of my black linen blazer. He and I were not a couple; we had only done it once, a few days before, when I had gone to his loft to look at his work. He showed me his current project, a series of photographs of a dead dog decaying in a vacant lot across the street from his place. He was going to call the series "Tribute to Martin Luther King" because he said King had been shot down like a dog. He told me that Woody Guthrie had a sticker on his guitar that said, *This Machine Kills Fascists.* Dennis said that, similarly, he considered his camera his rifle, his avenger. After we made love, he told me about the party. A lot of people were supposed to come, but his ex-girlfriend Sharon would be there. He said he didn't want to hurt her by flaunting me, but if I wanted to come to the party and hang loose, I would probably have a good time. When I got to the party, Dennis was talking to a blonde with legs up to her neck and Sharon, who I also knew from Max's, was standing at the food table, her face in the potato chips.

I stayed till two a.m., drinking tequila, dancing, smoking reefer, flirting, shaking my rump in Dennis's face, punishing him for hurting Sharon, for talking to blondes, for fucking me without falling in love with me. I was so cool; I didn't even speak to him. As I grabbed my blazer to go, he came over. "You look so fine dancing," he said. "How are you getting home? Why don't you wait for me outside? I'll be downstairs in ten minutes?"

"That's okay," I said. I went coolly out the door. He didn't know I had a gun in my pocket that made me invincible. It was a warm September night and I decided to walk home. People were still sitting out on the stoops, drinking and carrying on, passing around bottles of booze. I walked down through Park Slope, crossed Fulton Street, turned on to Cadman Plaza West in front of Borough Hall. I was heading south towards my building on the waterfront. The streets slowly became deserted and, as I walked down Old Fulton Street towards my building, I did not see a soul. My long hair streamed out behind me. I knew I was beautiful, the ruling Queen of Saturday night.

A man came up behind me so fast I didn't hear him. He grabbed me around the throat with a heavy arm and pushed something sharp into my cheek. I could see a broken, green bottle, the Heineken label still firmly attached. "We're going to have some fun," he said. He dragged me by the neck to an alley between two vacant warehouse buildings. He was twice my size and smelled of urine. He ripped open my blouse, knocked me to the ground, pulled my Indian print skirt off over my ankles and then rammed himself inside of me. "Does your boyfriend give it to you as good as this?" he asked. With the broken bottle he drew a line of blood across my chest from nipple to nipple, "Are you having fun?" he said.

My soul left my body and hovered in the air above us. I looked down and there was a couple having sex in an alley near some plastic bags full of garbage. The man covered the woman so completely that all I could see were her white knees glistening like stars. I thought about a game my ex-husband and I used to play called "Barbarian Horde." He would be Attila the Hun and I would be a ravishing but reluctantRoman courtesan. He would chase me from room to room, and I would flee before him, squealing, until finally, he caught me, threw me to the floor and gave me a rough pounding.

My soul returned to my body after the man pulled out of me. "If you ever tell anyone, I'll kill you," he said, and then he ran out of the alley.

I don't know how long I lay there. If I had not been so high, would I have heard him behind me, would I have whipped out my little gun and maced him into oblivion? Descartes said chance favors the prepared mind, but how can you guess the unforeseen?

I gathered my clothes around me. When I got inside my building, I woke up my downstairs neighbors, Joanne and George. They said I should go to the police right away. I said I couldn't. I had to lie down. I asked Joanne if she had any vinegar so I could douche; she said no, so I asked for Coca-Cola. "All we have is Heineken," she said. As I poured the beer into my douche bag, its rich smell reminded me how lucky I was to be alive.

Dennis's phone call woke me the next morning. I told him what had happened; thankfully, he did not say I told you so. He went with me to the police station where I was told that without evidence of semen in the vaginal tract, there was no proof that I had been raped. The scab across my chest was not enough. One of the detectives asked if my panties had been torn or stained. I didn't tell him I never wore panties. The police sent me to Kings County Hospital, where a kind Lebanese intern looked at the bruises on my thighs and the soreness in my vagina, sighed, and wrote on the report that despite the absence of semen, there was physical evidence to support my contention that I had been raped. He gave me some Valium and told me that, in his country, young women who were dishonored sometimes still kill themselves. Dennis stayed with me that night and held me in his arms. I pretended to be asleep, but I didn't sleep. A few days later he gave me a lovely gift, a leather folder to put my poems in.

I had learned the hard way that a gun will not keep you safe, and if you think you need a gun you are already in danger. The police never called to say they apprehended my assailant, so I guess they never did. I don't remember what happened to the little gun. Maybe I threw it in the East River. I don't like souvenirs.

How I Got My Apartment

Peter was uncircumcised and he showed me how to pull back the little cowl and clean the mucous-y stuff off the head of his cock with a washcloth. I could count the knots climbing up his spine; my private rosary, my prayer of pale flesh. I first saw him at the Easter Be-In. I had a yellow flower painted on my face. He was carrying a sketchpad and wearing a red and black plaid wool jacket. I didn't know then that red and black were the colors to wear on a vision quest. I was making my way through gone girls in granny skirts and would-be Maharishis in tie-dyed vests when I saw him and he saw me. We stopped and smiled at each other, standing about three feet apart, transfixed. He was so beautiful I thought he might be a mirage or some enchanted mannequin fallen from the clouds. When I blinked he was gone.

Two days later he appeared when I dropped in on some friends. That was when I knew there are no accidents. He asked me to go home with him. We walked over the Brooklyn Bridge to this building with a view of the Statue of Liberty from every window. In the morning he reached his long arm over to the easel beside the bed, picked up a paintbrush and drew a line down the center of my head, forever changing the part of my hair. He said he wanted to show me the desert and asked me to go to New Mexico with him.

I quit my job. We bought a truck at a Con Edison auction. At night he held me and told me about the Sangre De Christo Mountains, where breathing the air makes you high. He was my Jesus, my blue eyes, my boat across the Sea of Galilee. He taught me how to roll tobacco or reefer so I could roll while he drove. You make two little piles of flake inside the folded paper so the flake looks like a couple of mice swallowed by a snake, then you squash the little mice with your index finger and thumbs into a tight cylinder. We scored in Pittsburgh, Columbus, Chicago and St. Louis. We slept at truck stops. In the morning he would draw me, naked and rosy, lying on our piles of clothes. Out in the parking lot, truckers would walk by, joking and high on amphetamines and coffee. In New York he had bought me a low-cut peasant blouse with blue embroidered flowers on it and we made good use of it. All the way across Route 66, we looked for grocery and convenience stores with a man on duty behind the register. I would select a token loaf of bread, stuff the pockets of my loose denim skirt with cheese, lunch meats, little red boxes of raisins and go up to the check out counter. Then I would pull my peasant blouse down between my breasts and smile.

In Santa Fe he wanted to leave me. He said I was too emotional, talked to strangers about my feelings, wasn't cool. Then he sold a few drawings, decided to stay, made me sandals and a hashish pipe from the thighbone of a chicken. At the peyote rituals I waited with the Indian women outside the sweat lodge and when he stepped out I handed him an ear of corn. We met the Pranksters, got on the bus. Babs said I was good looking. Kesey traded Peter a sketch for a book, Gary Snyder's Rip Rap Poems. We lit out for the coast. I panhandled in Golden Gate Park while he sat drawing in the back of the truck. We got a job rolling marijuana cigarettes in chocolate papers for a wizard who sold them by the pack from a houseboat in Sausalito. Then we got a two-room pad on Potrero Hill. There was a window over the sink. While I washed the dishes, I could see the ships sail off to China.

I scavenged for our dinners in the dumpsters outside the Grand Union, where I met other stoned gleaners, gatherers for their tribes. He got a job as a shipping clerk, spent the money on rent and art supplies. We were happy. He shaved off all my pubic hair, then all his pubic hair, and we fucked as innocents. When the hair started to grow back, he shaved us again. But then he lost his job; I was too spaced to look for a job. We couldn't make the rent so we hit the road, drove south to L.A. where his German mother told me Jewish parents spoil their children, coddle them. I told her how I crawled through mountains of garbage to find a pack of stale English muffins to feed her son while he was sitting in our kitchen drawing pictures of rainbows.

Back on the road we quarreled. I said he had his drawing, his art. I wanted something of my own, a home, a baby. He answered: maybe later, when he was established, had a studio. I said, "Why does it always have to be what you want?" We drove back to New York and returned to this, his old building. We stayed with George on the second floor. My hair was down to the cleft in my ass and I got a job at Max's. I spent my tip money on groceries and cooked us vegetarian dinners. During the day he went foraging for reefer and acid. I was a lousy waitress, but no one seemed to notice. He wasn't drawing; he said he missed the desert.

One day he asked me if I had ever cheated on him. I don't know why, but I made up a long lie about how I met a guy named Brian when I was scavenging in the dumpsters. Brian took me to a black room, lit incense and candles and then drew cocaine flowers on my thighs. I told him I had gone to visit Brian in the black room several times. He slapped me so hard my jaw popped. "Brian must have loved you," he said. When I came home from work at four a.m. the next day, he and the truck were gone.

Later I found out he had gone across the street to the garage where Simon the sculptor lived, given him a blow job and borrowed 200 dollars. The next day, Franklin, the guy who lived on the top floor, told me he was moving to Germany to be with his lover Axel. He sold me this apartment with everything in it, for seventy-five dollars

Christmas

This Christmas, I want a miracle. I want to purge myself of cynicism and despair. I want to walk on water, grow the wings of an angel, learn to sing on key, and always be joyful in the company of friends. I don't want a little plaster crêche with a tiny plaster baby Jesus or a plastic tree: I want peace on Earth and the Star of Bethlehem.

My Jewish mother told me that Jesus was not the son of God because if he were the son of God and had walked on the earth the Holocaust could not have happened. She said we were still waiting for the Savior. If I kept looking out the window I might see him coming up the street on the shoulders of F.D.R. and my dead grandpa Max.

I was not so easily appeased. I wanted Christmas and a larger, more mysterious world than the one she defended with her vacuum cleaner and old wives tales. I wanted the wine and the wafer, the blood and the body, and everything else I did not know, so I started to hang out with the Irish boys from Gerritson Beach.

One Christmas night I went with Dennis Keith Patrick O'Malley into the back seat of his father's parked Plymouth Fury and showed him my rosy new breasts. He made me come with his fingers; then I rubbed the hard bulge under his black chinos until it flattened and grew moist beneath my hand. Suddenly he turned from me, sat up, crossed himself, and said, "Mea culpa, mea culpa, mea maxima culpa." I asked him what that meant, but he would not tell me. Later I found out it meant that he was ashamed.

I could not understand this puzzling connection between pleasure and shame. I tried wilder Gerritson beach boys, crazy ones, drag racers, arsonists, but they were so ashamed of themselves they had to carve their initials on their forearms with razor blades to remember their names. I always knew who I was, a would-be adventurer, a midget Rockette with more imagination than legs, trying to kick the moon. I grew muscles on both sides of my tongue and learned to give phenomenal blowjobs so I would always be the one in control.

Eventually, I found out I didn't like being in control — it was too much responsibility. I wanted to be the baby, the one who was taken care of. I also wanted a baby so I could control it, but I was too selfish to give over my body so another soul could grow. I wanted to escape my skin and find salvation in the Christian world, but I could not accept the idea of original sin or feel ashamed of how I prayed in the garden of my body. My sex was the only thing about myself I could trust.

I married a longhaired, hippie desperado who turned out to be a mama's boy. I left him and married him in different forms again and again. Finally I learned I would not find Deus Ex Machina in the arms of mortal men, but I still want Christmas and virgin births and peace on Earth because I want to believe that bread is holy and God is love.

My neighbor Mary says I should get a dog, but they are too needy and often have bad breath. I am lonely, past menopause, too old to have a baby and now I regret my barrenness. At night I pile my bed with books and pour through them until my eyes are red looking for instructions on how to accept the fact that I am already an extinct species. Is the message of Christmas that the only hope is in acceptance? Kafka says no. Buddha and Bukowski say yes, have some eggnog, spread your legs.

My brother sent me a computer for Christmas but I have not yet unpacked it because it terrifies me. I went to hear a brilliant, young philosopher lecture on artificial intelligence. He said computers are more logical than people, and that being able to understand the essence of a zebra, as computers do, is more important than actually being able to see a zebra. Being able to understand the essence of another life would truly be a miracle for me. I can't understand my own life. Is being able to understand the essence of another life what love is? Maybe I should get a zebra and see, or better yet become a bone marrow donor or give a kidney or rib and in that way survive in the body of another after the end of this, my illogical, biological life. Then I would be a holy ghost indeed.

The Year in Review

In the last year, I dyed my hair blonde so many times that it fell out. Now if you look at the top of my head, it looks like a chicken's. However, I am not a chicken but many animals, a fox, a squirrel, a tiger and a wombat in the same body. This year the wombat has been in power. Night after night I stay awake burrowing around in my head trying to push out the damp soil, the mold. I am trying to relinquish the concept of linear time because I don't want to find myself living a life of diminishing returns. I don't want to be trapped by regrets or stopped because of a disappointment in love; when I am hurt I climb back into the walls of my tunnel. I don't want to see my friends.

I was knitting my best male friend a black turtleneck sweater for Christmas. My plan was to give him the sweater, tell him my feelings for him had deepened and take him to bed. Before I even had a chance to attach the sleeves to the body he told me he had fallen for a woman. He said he loved me like a sister but couldn't imagine us having sex. He hoped I would be happy that he had met someone.

It might be easier for me to be happy for him if that someone were not one of my friends. I will unravel this sweater and follow the twisted wool out of this mess. Maybe I will go out into the street, hail a taxi and have an affair with the driver. If I can't find a taxi, I will look for a policeman or a man who works in a bodega. I find the prospect of an affair with a man with a dangerous occupation exciting. Every time we do it may be the last, so we will take special care. If I do not find a man with a dangerous occupation, I will come back upstairs, pick up my journal for this year, leaf through the pages, look for signs of progress, and relive joyful events.

My nephew Matthew's pointed head makes him look like a little Yoda. One night Matthew woke up the household with his crying. My brother was rocking him in his arms, carrying him around the living room but Matthew kept crying. When my brother glanced out the window, he saw two men in the driveway; they had already pried open the door of the family car. When my brother turned on the house lights, the men ran away. Maybe we have a psychic baby in the family.

This is the year I started to write every day. I get up in the morning, drink three cups of coffee with milk and honey, and then go to my typewriter. If what I write is painful, I don't get up and space out, drink more coffee or shave my legs. I force myself to sit here and pull the pain out through my fingers onto the typewriter keys. This is forward motion and I know it is changing me for the better. When the writing is going well, I feel like helium, lighter than air. Unfortunately I have developed a pain in my left side, which my Chinese herbalist says will go away if I stop drinking coffee. But I don't want to give up coffee; I would rather give up toilet paper.

This year I slept with a thirty-year-old man who told me he was twenty-four the morning after. Eventually he stopped calling. This year I lived on so little money that it was a treat to buy the newspaper. I don't know how many times he called me, I stopped picking up when I heard his voice.

This year I reconciled with my friend Annette Planet, the astrologer, from whom I had been estranged for two years. I am happy we are speaking again and she has promised not to call me up and make predictions. I don't want to know the future. I like working blind, foraging through the night for roots and bark like a wombat. I still feel bad because my dear friend does not want to be my lover, but wombats have little use for self-pity.

On my birthday this year, I went to Brighton Beach and let the ocean wash the bitterness out of my heart. I would do that today except that it is the end of December and it is raining. Maybe I will clean out my closets and go through my drawers looking for a magic snake to carry me into the New Year. When I find him coiled in a crate of books or hiding under my one good white silk shirt, I will call him out, watch him dance in the murky light that illuminates my life, and let the serpent beguile me.

National Security

I look at my bare ass by looking backwards over my shoulder into the mirror on my bathroom door. I am pleased. My ass is large but not saggy, still shapely, prosperous, the most substantial thing about me. This is an ass that says here is a woman who knows how to sit on a barstool, she likes a good meal and she loves to dance. She has fat to burn and is willing, but you'd better respect this ass because if you don't it will crush you. I will sit on your face and not get up. Struggling to breathe through my dense flesh, you will be pressed back into the pillows, trapped, and you will know that you are going down, death by derriere.

My ass is my secret weapon, although it is so prominent it is not much of a secret. My ass could teach the current administration a thing or two because it does not equivocate. Maybe if I show the President my ass he will proclaim it a national treasure, have it carved on Mt. Rushmore next to Lincoln's nose.

The first time I ever let a man stick it in my ass. He told me that whenever he thought about ass fucking he thought about me. He said my plump ass, with its two dimples on either cheek, was the most beautiful he had ever seen. He said he had never done it that way either and that we would be virgins together in the only way we could be virgins together. He was an all night, all right man. I trusted him, so I let him, it was fine.

That was one time when I knew whom to trust; nowadays I might as well consult the intestines of goats; but I am not alone, everyone is afraid to trust. We are drowning ourselves in bottles of Absolut and blowing each other away with Smith and Wessons and 357 Magnums because we don't know whom to trust. Gun control laws are all well and good but, just like when I bleached my hair blond because I thought it would keep people from noticing the lines in my neck, it's working from the outside in, ass-backwards, a temporary panacea for an epidemic of fear.

Not that I'm any more secure than any one else, I'm a wreck, I'm dirty laundry, I'm shredded wheat. I telephone a lady poet whom I thought was my friend. As soon as she heard my voice she said, "Oh, it's you."

I said, "Hi, how are you doing?"

She said, "I don't want to talk to you now."

I said, "When should I call you?"

She said, "Don't, I'll call you."

Maybe she is jealous because her ass is not as substantial as mine. When she calls I'll tell her all she needs is a dozen cheese danishes and several margaritas, that will fix her ass right up. I think back over our last few conversations and realize she only calls when she wants something, access to my pot connection or the name of my editor at *Downtown.*

Alas, she is not really my friend. The next time she asks me for something I will tell her to kiss my ass. At least with an ass like mine I have a cushion on which to sit and meditate. I sink to the floor, assume the lotus pose; perhaps I can access Alpha. I take long, deep, slow breaths and silently recite like a mantra the names of people I can trust; my brother Joel, my friend Laurie, my friends Margo, Jan, Ed and Ursula. The faces of several other people float into my mind and I match each face with its right name. I know I am very lucky to have these good friends to count on, then I think about my mother and father and my breathing immediately becomes more shallow and labored.

My mother is crippled with arthritis and bursitis because she has never been able to allow herself to relax. My father has mysterious pains in his chest despite his new heart valve. I can trust them to love me completely, blindly, because they think I am theirs, but whenever I expect them to understand me I only nuke myself. I try to forgive them for their limitations, maybe the limitations are mine. Maybe I have a bug up my ass, or even worse, a little mouse gnawing at my entrails and I will become so weak I won't be able to trust anyone. Then my ass will really be cooked. My mind wanders away and I see myself crouched over a crack pipe in a doorway on Avenue D., a few grimy shopping bags at my feet stuffed with tattered poems.

Now I am too restless to continue meditation. I get off my big ass, which is just as well because here I am with no bloomers on, my ass dusty from my dirty floor, I hear strange voices in the hall. I look over and notice once again that I forgot to lock the door.

Persephone

In the Underworld, the souls of heroes roam the gray meadows of Aspodel and wander beside the palace of Hades and Persephone, his reluctant bride. Next to the palace are two pools of clear water; to the left is the pool of Lethe, forgetfulness, where the common souls, carping and twittering like bats, flock to drink. Initiated souls avoid this pond and drink instead from the pool at the right, the pool of memory. The waters of memory are bitter, permeated with the gritty sands of disappointment, but it is said that if you can drink the water of memory down you will gain immortality of the soul. I want to become one of the initiates, ingest my bitter memories and learn from my failures. I want to die with my eyes open, a smile on my face, giving the "V" for victory sign, but so often I choose the pond of forgetfulness.

The man who takes my elbow when we cross the street and has size thirteen feet tells me he has finally broken up with his girlfriend; then I see them embracing passionately in Tompkins Square Park. I flee to the Right Bank, my favorite bar in Williamsburg, where I get soused on sake, rub my body shamelessly against every man at the bar, and finally bring home a twenty-six-year old painter named Ali who refuses to make love to me: what he really wants is to try on my clothes. I have to literally push him out the door. The weight of my own vulnerability makes me feel like I am carrying a big, ugly, dead dog around my neck. I go to the refrigerator where there is a third of a bottle of Absolut left over from the night before. I suck it down into my desperate throat. I wake up on my kitchen floor sweating and filled with rage.

My friend Alice has been getting harassing phone calls for the last six months. She goes to the police and finds out that there is a harassment unit because complaints of this nature are epidemic. An Officer Logan is assigned to her case; he traces the calls to a forty-eight-year-old man whom she used to date and who still lives with his mother. She dropped him when she found out he was a virgin. I commiserate with Alice, but all the time I am thinking about the fates I have imagined for men who rejected me. I wanted to change them into rats, cockroaches, earthworms.

I get a postcard with a picture of a nasty witch on it from a woman who has delusions that she is a feminist. The caption on the other side reads "This is how you look." Maybe so, but I wish she had the courage to call me up so we could discuss our differences directly. I wonder if, when people don't confront their anger and rage directly, they strike out in terrible bizarre ways. They become child molesters, wife beaters, alcoholics or drug addicts and try to drown themselves in the pool of forgetfulness.

I read in the newspaper that John Wayne Gacy has received more than 27,000 letters, some of these from women who want to marry him. Never mind that he has been convicted of dismembering and killing dozens of young boys and men. Who are these women, who write to him, these women who are my sisters in vulnerability, desperation, shame?

Persephone was frolicking with a group of maidens in a meadow when she wandered off, entranced by the fragrance of a flowering narcissus on the wind. She ran across the meadow to gather a bouquet. Her face and arms buried in blossoms, she did not notice Hades, the God of the Underworld, ride up behind her in his chariot drawn by coal-black horses. He seized her by the wrist and carried her off to his underground kingdom, where he raped her and took her for his bride. If Persephone had not been so entranced by the beauty of the Narcissus, she might have heard Hades behind her and changed herself into a tree or a rock. The Austrian poet, Georg Trakl, says that those who love true beauty are forever given into Death's hand. No wonder the Goddess of Spring, Persephone, is also called Core, the Goddess of Death.

I have always been a sucker for grace, beauty, and a pretty face. The man who quotes Shakespeare in bed finally calls me up and invites me to dinner in a Thai restaurant. I do not refuse, although I haven't heard from him in a month. He looks like a cross between Tom Cruise and young Lawrence Olivier.

We have a wonderful time and the next night he calls me to say he wants to come over at dawn, which is after work for him. He drives a taxi. He arrives bringing me a peanut butter cookie and a copy of *The Times* with the crossword puzzle partially done.

For 59-Down, which asks for a four letter word for a false god, he has written idol. This reminds me that, when I fall for someone, I put him up on a pedestal; then we both wind up going through hell.

I don't want this to happen with the man who quotes Shakespeare in bed. We stand at my window and watch first light break over the cherry trees blossoming in the park across the street. He strips, pulls my nightgown off over my head, and takes me in his arms. I can feel the rhythm of his beating heart. He does not say a word as he carries me to bed. I seat myself on top of him. Once again, I am Persephone, unable to stop myself, running breathless through the meadow drawn by the scent of narcissus on the wind.

Scrotums

I like to think of a man's scrotum tucked away neatly in the surrounding bed of hair or flapping long and loose as he rises from my bed and goes into the kitchen to get us another beer. I like to think of my lovers' scrotums and all men's scrotums as magic carpets or sacred places. I believe that within the scrotum lies the access code to eternal life. I am not comfortable around women who do not love men or who blame men for their own unhappiness; maybe I am making up my own feminism as I climb the twisted road of my own existence.

Sometimes I stop at an interesting plateau, named Kevin or Michael, where the vegetation is lush and intriguing, where I hope to linger and refresh myself with a new (to me) and exotic variety of the fruit of life. Sometimes I read a book, often a book of Allen Ginsberg's poetry because I sense he also lives in this fashion, climbing and climbing and climbing, then pausing for refreshment and reflection, then shouldering his pack of delusory hope and smartass self-deprecation before going on, but I often worry about Ginsberg and wonder what, in his journey from iconoclast to icon, he has had to leave behind.

Did he throw away his old, torn B.V.D's or his dog-eared copy of the *Kama Sutra*? Is he wearing paisley cotton boxer shorts today and is his scrotum, which I imagine was once oily and smelled like limburger cheese, now as plump and rosy as a tenured persimmon? A man can compose his face, put on a confident smile or a grimace of disdain, but a scrotum is something else again and may present a better portrait of a man's character.

I have found that men with taut, little scrotums, the kind that hold the testes together like two peanuts in a shell, only tip five percent, while men with loose, bulbous scrotums come quickly and then like to cuddle for hours. I have found that men with many visible blue veins cross-hatching their scrotums are the ones with velvet tongues that tickle me like 10,000 fingers, as does Ginsberg's poetry when he calls himself a "cocksucker, a decay, a talking lust, a creep in the eyes of the universe." But when I read in the newspaper that he is co-chairing a panel discussion at N.Y. U. on "The Beat Generation in American Prophecy" that cost fifty dollars to get into, all I can think is Oh, Boddhidharma, where are your dancing shoes now?

It may be inevitable that today's iconoclasts become the icons of tomorrow, who will in turn be shattered by kids in sneakers shooting baskets or twelve-year-old computer hackers. Maybe in twenty-five years I'll be doing American Express commercials, but it is more likely I will be eating crusts of pizza out of garbage cans unless I can parlay my fascination with scrotums into a best seller. Maybe I should write a book, *Scrotums of the Beats,* and interview Caroline Cassady, or maybe I should become a photographer and do a photo essay, "Beat Balls — The Survivors" and photograph the testes of William Burroughs and Lawrence Ferlinghetti, but my best chance of success would be to get a handle on my own obsessive behavior long enough to do some sustained work.

Whenever I let a man into my life, I become too frantic to do yoga, my writing schedule is shot to smithereens and I terrify him with my obsessive desire. My lover, the man who quotes Shakespeare in bed, has a scrotum that tastes like a peach. When I see him flirting with another woman in the bar, I pass him a note that says, "You blew it." He comes over and says he is glad this happened now and not two years down the line and gives me back my keys. He is not answering his phone and I cannot stop flagellating myself because I am not the Buddha. When I close my eyes all I can see is the strong clean line of his back bending over.

My friend Jan tells me it is now or never, get professional help, go see a psychiatrist, a headshrinker. I tell her I don't need a headshrinker, in the last three days my head has shrunk to the size of a pea. I say I must be with him again and that I wish I was a pimple on his scrotum. I tell Jan that what I need is to consult a visionary, a mystic what to do is summon up Walt Whitman or William Blake.

I pick my copy of Ginsberg's Collected Poems: 1947 to 1980 and see that on page 235 there is a poem, "I Beg You, Come Back and Be Cheerful." I turn to that page and read, "what if the worlds were a series of steps, what if the steps joined back at the margin leaving us flying like birds into time." I decide to call Ginsberg up right away and ask him if he is willing to share what knowledge he has about combating the ogres of obsessive behavior. I know he lives on the lower east side of Manhattan but not exactly where. When I pick up my Manhattan phone directory, I see that there is an Aaron, an Achmed and an Aristotle Ginsberg listed, but alas no Allen.

Theseus

I feel haggard and worn and I want to be a virgin again. I steam my pudenda clean at the Tenth Street Baths and come home and anoint it with oil of gardenia. I pick up a copy of Robert Graves' *Greek Myths,* because it cheers me to read about heroic deeds of valor. Then I climb into bed with a cheap bottle of Gallo red and a substantial chunk of hashish given to me by my old friend Didi. She can afford to be generous because she has made a killing in the last year. She has patented a cunning leather thigh strap for dildos that allows two women to penetrate each other simultaneously.

I tell her she should call it the Girdle of Aphrodite; she says she likes the jockstrap of Venus better and that it renders men unnecessary. While this may be the Holy Grail for some, I don't want to render men anything but pleasure while they render me the same in equal measure. I put the hash in my old wooden pipe and think that if I were a virgin again, I would not walk off, as I did at fifteen, with the first flashy lounge lizard that tells me I am beautiful. I'd wait for a gentle boy with strong fingers who sings me songs; about Hercules and the golden apples of the Hesperides and Theseus who killed the Minotaur and loved danger for its own sake. Maybe I'll even stay with the gentle boy, grow old with him. The phallocentric culture in which I live says I'm already old at fifty and should be thinking about facelifts and cemetery plots, but I prefer to think of anal sex with me on top and swimming in the sparkling ocean.

Maybe I'll swim out so far I'll find the lost island of Atlantis and build condominiums or maybe I'll catch the maniacs that kill taxi drivers, just like the great hero Theseus caught the bandits that beset helpless travelers. In any case, I'll rest here and dream that I am strong enough to rise above my current misfortunes. Ever since my ex-lover, the man who quotes Shakespeare in bed, gave me back my keys, I feel like Prometheus chained to the mountain with an eagle pecking at my liver. I thought I was as tough as Pallas Athena, Goddess of the Hunt, but once I fell for him I acted like a craven nymphomaniac when he wouldn't give me his big thunderbolt. I surrendered my power to him, although he didn't ask for it, didn't want it, and now I cannot allow myself to hope that Hercules will come along and save me.

I don't know if power is an absolute like a rock or an invisible flame with a soul of its own that scorches you in order to test you. The president of the National Organization for Women says that rape is not about sex, it's about power. Maybe they are the same, a monster with many faces like Cerebrus, the fifty-headed dog that stands at the gates of hell. The Tibetan Buddhists say chastity is the parent of all human happiness but I devoutly hope not. All the same, maybe the next time I fall for someone I will be able to maintain my self-respect.

As I draw on the pipe, I think that maybe I got hysterical because the man who quoted Shakespeare in bed always insisted on being the one to initiate sex. It is as if Ariadne suddenly appeared and offered me a ball of magic thread to guide me out of the labyrinth. I remember how he would come to my place, open the refrigerator door, take out a beer and then ask me if I had any reefer. If I did I would say yes; now I realize he never had any to share. Didi says the affair was doomed because he was half my age and that I am a love addict and should go to Co-Dependents Anonymous meetings. I tell her I'd rather read Robert Graves and that I will always love danger and go for the possibility of triumphing over impossible odds.

Theseus spent his youth with his mother in southern Greece. When it was time for him to go to his father in Athens, a ship was placed at his disposal, but he refused to go by water because the voyage was safe and easy. He dreamed of becoming a great hero, so he set off on foot and killed all the bandits he met on the road. By the time he got to Athens, the citizens were singing his praises. I puff on the pipe once more and as I watch the smoke rise higher and higher, I know that even if I could be a virgin again I would not choose safe passage by water. My way is ordeal by fire.

The Book of Life

When I was seven, my mother told me that when my parents decided on a name for me, my grandfather went to the temple and told the rabbi my name, Tsaurah. First the rabbi said a special naming prayer for me, and then he entered my name in the Book of Life.

"Where is the book?" I wanted to know. I wanted to see my name on the page. I wanted to know who came before and who came after. My only childhood friend, Debra Maloney, was Catholic; I wanted to see her name in the book, too. The book must be as big as the ocean, I thought. "Where," I asked my mother, "does the rabbi keep it?" My mother told me that the Book of Life was not a real book, but an imaginary book, a pretend book. I would not find Debra's name in it because Catholics do not believe in books; they name babies by dripping water on their heads. I knew this was too ridiculous to be true; besides I wanted God to write in the Book of Life that Debra Maloney would be my friend forever.

"What good is a book if you can't read it?" I cried.

"You don't have to read the Book of Life," she said. "You just have to know it's there."

"The rabbi must know where it is," I argued. "He has to in order to write my name in it."

"I am your mother," she said, her voice going shrill. "Would ever I lie to you? Now listen carefully. In the naming prayer, the Rabbi speaks to God and God writes your name in the Book of Life." Then she tried to buy me off with a glass of her special chocolate milk, but I refused. I was beginning to suspect this God of hers was a jokester and a meany, pretending to write in an imaginary book, and even worse, sending poor Daniel into the lion's den and Jonah into the belly of a whale.

I have since learned you can read an imaginary book with the eye of your imagination and I have come to agree with Kierkegaard that if there is a God, it is hope. I was fifty-one years old last week and I am glad that I am still in the Book of Life. I have lived many lives in this one. I have been a fool, a joker, a servant, a beggar, a knave, a queen, a slut, and a pompous ass, and yet it seems as if I've just gotten started.

Sometimes false pride rules me, sometimes rampant insecurity. On my birthday, I wake up feeling anxious and freaked out because my new lover, Ace, has not called in five days, nor has he responded to messages I left on his answering machine. I get up out of bed, eat four spoons of honey straight from the jar in an effort to get high and shift my focus off of him. However, I continue to obsess.

I know he was not killed in a car crash because yesterday I drove by where he works and his car was where he always parks it. My friend Jayne says there must be a logical explanation: my phone number is unlisted, perhaps he has lost it; but then I want to know why he has not come by and thrown pebbles up at my window. Jayne says I am a hopeless masochist. The last time Ace and I spent the night with each other, I tied his ankles together with my white push-up bra. He looked dismayed, but then I mounted him and started us on a galloping ride. "Don't stop, don't stop," he moaned, his whole body shaking with pleasure. Maybe he was faking it, maybe he really didn't have a good time, or maybe he is now scuba diving under the lost continent of Atlantis. I can't understand why he has abandoned me. I am so despondent I don't want to go to the beach, as I do every year on my birthday to put my body in the ocean at exactly my natal time: 4:23 p.m. I make an effort and force myself into last year's too-tight bathing suit, which leaves half my ass sticking out. I pull on a sweatshirt and jeans, put a couple of towels in my backpack and I'm off.

On the subway I torment myself by thinking about how nice it would have been to have seen Ace on my birthday, to have made love. At the beach I park my towel next to the towel of a young Russian couple playing Frisbee. It starts to rain but they continue to play. I strip to my suit. It's 4:20 by my watch: now or never. I wade in through the choppy, breaking waves, take the plunge, and, in my awkward crawl, strike out for another world. I swim until I am breathless. Turning on my back in the salty brine, I am an embryo floating in the cradle of time. All my worries wash away in the white foam.

On my way back to the subway I stop in a ninety-nine-cent store on Brighton Beach Avenue and buy a blue candle to light in the hope that it will make Ace call me.

When I get home there is a message on my answering machine. My stomach flip-flops when I see the blinking red light. I hope it is Ace, but it is my mother wishing me Happy Birthday and inviting me down to Maryland for Labor Day. "We can celebrate your birthday and Rosh Hashanah comes on Labor Day this year. You can come to temple with us," she says.

Why not? I think, I have nothing better to do, and I have not been inside a synagogue for fifteen years. My parents go to a reform temple that looks like a McDonald's with a big neon Star of David on top. Perhaps the rabbi of such an establishment would be willing to reveal the location of the Book of Life. I call my friend Ursula, who has a spare set of my keys. I ask her to come over and water my plants. I give her my parents' and my brother's phone numbers in case of emergencies.

My father meets me at the train station wearing his Baltimore Orioles cap and a needy smile. His bony legs protrude from a pair of too-large yellow Bermuda shorts that make him look like an oversized chicken. When we hug I think I can feel the scar on his chest over his plastic heart valve. "How did an ugly guy like me get such a beautiful daughter?" he asks. On the drive to my brother's, where the rest of the family waits to celebrate my birthday, my father talks nonstop about the different kinds of insurance policies he and my mother are considering that pay for in-home nursing care in case of catastrophic illness. Then he says he wants to put some of his assets in my name. I want to change the tone of this conversation so I say, "Maybe I will take the money and run off to New Zealand. I hear there are gorgeous men there."

"Are you kidding?" he asks. "Is that some kind of joke? You're fifty-one years old! You should be responsible by now." I am tempted to ask, "Why? Will being responsible save me from a plastic heart valve?"

Instead I ask if he went to temple when my nephew Matthew was born last year to put Matthew's name in the Book of Life. "Yes," my father answers, "now it cost a hundred bucks. When Grandpa did it for you it was only ten."

At my brother's house, my mother kisses me. She whispers in my ear, "Happy Birthday. How does it feel to know your life is more than half-over?" When I tell her that is a terrible thing to say, she says, "I didn't mean anything, dear."

My brother Joel says, "Hi, toots." My sister-in- law Judi gives me a hug, and my five-year-old niece Julia runs into my arms. Matthew, who has just started to walk, takes a few hesitant steps in my direction. He is adorable, a platinum blonde with very dark eyes like mine. My brother tells me Matthew is talking now and can say three words; Ma, foop and ding. Foop is food and whenever they are preparing food or getting ready to eat Matthew gets excited and waves his arms around yelling "foop, foop, foop." The word ding is for the ringing of the telephone and my brother says, "It's weird how Matthew starts yelling ding, ding, ding, just before the phone rings." We discuss the possibility of Matthew being psychic; first his crying during the attempted robbery and now this. I suggest that when he grows up he can make money by channeling Elvis. "Very funny," my brother responds, and then "foop, foop, foop," yells Matthew as Judi brings a huge platter of steamed crabs to the dining room table. My mother straps Matthew into his high chair and we all sit down to a birthday dinner in my honor.

After the dishes have been cleared Judi and Julia disappear into the kitchen and come back with a big chocolate cake that they have baked for me. As I blow out the single candle on the cake, I wish for true love. The cake squishes and crumbles beneath the knife as I am cutting it.

"Have Joel cut the cake," my mother says. "He knows how to cut a cake."

"I can cut my own cake," I say. My mother tells her friends that I am a writer, something like Danielle Steele, but she has never forgiven me for not fulfilling the dreams she had for me. She can not understand why my brother, a B- student, has a palatial home on three acres while I, her child prodigy with the genius I.Q., can barely afford the rent of my two-room apartment with cockroaches.

After dinner, on the drive to my parents' home where I will spend the night, my mother asks if I have any readings coming up. "Yes," I tell her, "I will be reading my work in two weeks at the performance space ABC No Rio. It's the most famous performance space on the Lower East Side."

"But you don't get paid," my mother says.

"Yes, I do." I reply. "They pass the hat."

"That's all you get," my mother says, "spare change."

I blow up and start yelling at her. "You should be happy people want to come hear me read! Nothing I do is ever good enough for you! You don't understand me or respect me!"

"I didn't mean anything, dear," my mother says.

"Yes, you did," I yell. "You meant to make me feel bad about myself so you could feel superior."

"Girls, girls," my father breaks in. "Stop it! You're making me sick. My chest hurts. I'm having pains."

"Here Jerry," my mother says. "Take a Valium." She rummages through the many vials of pills she always carries in her handbag, like amulets to ensure that she and my father will continue in the Book Of Life. She finds the proper vial, extracts a yellow pill, and hands it to my father. He swallows it. We ride through the night not speaking, like strangers on a train, as we have done many times before.

My parent's home is a four-room condo in a high-rise jutting up incongruously out of the rolling Maryland hills. As I am brushing my teeth, my mother comes in and tells me that she and my father have finally decided to buy that special kind of insurance from John Hancock Insurance Company.

She says that they do not want to be a burden to my brother and me. I stop bushing my teeth and manage a thank you. I know it is the right thing to say, I make a move to embrace her but she has already turned away.

My parents' efforts to settle their affairs and prepare for their final stage of life are gallant and touching, but I wish they would take their money and go off to Tahiti or at least Miami Beach. I lie in a cot in my mother's sewing room, but of course I cannot sleep. My mother's steady snoring echoes through the silent apartment. My father moans and rolls, thrashing around in the bedcovers.

"Leah," he calls out, "Leah." My mother's name is Ruth.

In the morning my mother asks what pieces I would like to have from her collection of antique Chinese porcelains. "I want you to have the first pick," she says and I know she is trying to make amends. I choose a big rose medallion teapot. "That's my favorite too," she says, smiling. Under the crosshatched lines that cover her cheeks I see my young mother, her beauty, her fine, shining face.

That evening we go to the reform temple with golden twin arches over the entrance that make it look like McDonald's. As we enter several people look over at me in my black miniskirt, black tights and combat boots, but my parents flank me proudly and introduce me to their friends. We take seats.

"In the year 5757," the rabbi addresses his congregation from the podium made of what looks like blue plastic. "Try to be better Jews.

God is a sun," he adds, "and he that lives with his back to the sun will spend a life in shadows." I recognize this as a quote from Kalil Gilbran but the rabbi does not mention that he is quoting the famous mystic. Later in his sermon, while talking about the Arab-Israeli situation, the rabbi says, "Something there is that does not love a wall, that wants it down," quoting Robert Frost. He does not give Frost credit either.

The cantor is a redheaded woman who plays the ukulele and harmonica, but mercifully not at the same time. I do not like the meek supplicant quality of the prayers and do not read along until we get to the part where we give thanks for the last year. Then, I surprise myself as I join the congregation and pray to be included in the Book of Life for the year to come. My father has started to cry and I take his hand, which is dry and thin. My mother is pretending not to notice my father's tears or my attempt to comfort him because public displays of emotion terrify her. It strikes me as amazing, that after all we have been through, the joy, treachery, lies, disappointments, and misunderstandings, we have somehow arrived at an uneasy truce. This allows us to be here together, here in prayer. Given the wavy gravy course of my life thus far, this minor miracle is as miraculous as the parting of the Red Sea.

The rabbi is standing at the door shaking hands as we file out of the temple. My father introduces me as his daughter from New York, the published writer. The rabbi shakes my hand enthusiastically and then I ask him, "Where is the Book of Life?" He looks startled, drops my hand, steps back. "I don't know," he says, then thinks for a second. "In God's library," he counters, proving he is a comedian as well as a plagiarist.

We drive to my brother's for dinner. As my five-year-old niece and I are setting the table she tells me I have not folded the napkins straight and am putting the knife on the wrong side. I wonder if she will grow up to be like my mother, who is sitting with Matthew playing with building blocks on the living room floor. All of a sudden Matthew stands up and starts turning around in circles. "Ding, ding, ding," he yells. My brother, who is entering the room with an armful of dishes, gives me a look, and the next minute the phone rings. My sister-in-law brings in the phone.

"It's for you," she says.

"Hello," I say.

I hear Ace say in his rich Brooklyn accent, "Hey babe, I lost your number. I went by your house a coupla times but you weren't home; then I ran into Ursula and she gave me your brother's number. Happy Birthday."

Sleeping with the Enemy

My lover Ace does not like the twentieth century; he wants to live in the days of the Old West, when every man owned a gun, ornery blacks were lynched as a matter of course, the law was the fastest man on the draw and women were soft and gentle. I point out to him that women didn't stay soft and gentle for very long. One out of four died in childbirth. Many others started having children at thirteen and were worn-out hags by the time they were thirty. I tell him he doesn't really know what it was like in the Old West. He has swallowed the romantic pap of TV westerns. He says he hates to fight with me, let's not talk about politics and suggests a ride on his motorcycle. I bite my tongue until it bleeds and then say yes.

We go to Nathan's in Coney Island for cheese fries and then walk down the boardwalk to Brighton Beach where we sit on a bench near the end of the boardwalk. On either side of us sit old people sunning themselves. Since it is Simchat Torah, a Jewish high holy day, whole families stroll by in their holiday best. Snatches of Russian and Yiddish float on the breeze. I remember when I was a child and we lived with my grandparents they would speak in Russian when they didn't want anyone to know what they were saying.

"I don't like Russian Jews," Ace says, interrupting my memories.

"What?" I ask, shocked. "You know I am a Russian Jew!"

"But you were born here," he says. "And besides, you are not loud and pushy like them. You are soft and gentle."

I am momentarily speechless; then I manage to sputter out, "Even though I am American, and agnostic at that, I am still of Jewish descent and that can never change."

"You have some funny ideas in your pretty little head," he tells me.

I am so furious I cannot speak as we walk back down the boardwalk and ride to my place. He wants to come up, but I manage to mumble that I have work to do. I am hurt, appalled and fuming.

That night, I have a dream. In the dream I am in an anonymous bedroom. I turn away from the sleeping form of the man beside me, and, reaching for the bottle of Scotch on the bedside table, see his things in a jumble on the floor; his shining leather boots, beige jodhpurs, a revolver and a thick, black coiled whip. As I watch, the whip uncoils and becomes a snake, spitting and hissing. It rises, poised to strike at my eyes. At this point I wake up shivering in my bed and covered with goose bumps.

This snake dream is an old dream, as familiar to me as a song learned in childhood. I used to dream it when I lived with Michael Frank, a lover who went to massage parlors and paid other women for sex. I know I cannot stay with Ace, but when he calls me up three days later and suggests a motorcycle ride out to Bay Ridge and a fish dinner, I accept. I think maybe if we talk I can get him to see how insidious his thinking is, but when he shows up with a metal swastika on a leather thong around his neck I explode. I call him a racist moron and say I never want to see him again. I run around my apartment grabbing his shaving things from the bathroom, his spare shirt and socks from my lingerie drawer, thrust them into his arms.

"What are you, crazy? You on the rag?" he calls out as I shove him through the door.

The truth is that I knew what he was like from the start. On our first date, somewhere between the Caesar salad and the steak, he told me he didn't like Blacks. Later that evening as we were driving into Manhattan to see a movie, he asked me to get another pack of smokes from the glove compartment and I saw the gun.

"Is this real?" I asked.

"Sure, it's real," he said.

"What's it for?" I wanted to know.

"In case some trouble arises," he said. "With so many undesirables around, you never know what will happen."

But I still let him kiss me that night and two dates later I took him into my bed and shared it with him again and again. Maybe because of my loneliness and desperation or maybe I liked how his breath always smelled like Camel cigarettes and his skin tasted like milk. Perhaps the truth was that, at last, I had become totally depraved. I was doing it again and again with a man who embodied the worst of the culture I struggle against, a man who refused to acknowledge my anger, my pain, who insisted on seeing me as soft and gentle when I am furious and deranged. What could be more perverse, more dirty? Autoerotic strangulation? Necrophilia?

When I tell my friend Jane how disgusted I feel that I was ever involved with Ace, she says I am being too hard on myself: I was alone and vulnerable. He was virile and persistent. My mother is always telling me that I can't keep a man because I don't know how to compromise, but at what point does compromise become collusion, capitulation, catastrophe? I would rather sleep alone than make a bargain with the devil. I wonder if this happened because I am getting old, losing my courage. Perhaps, one day, I will no longer have the strength to be fierce and vigilant. Maybe I should take steroids or inject the gonads of bulls into my head.

When French President Mitterrand admitted his collaboration with the Vichy government, fifty-three percent of the French citizens who were asked what would have happened if this was known when he first campaigned for office said that they would have voted for him anyway. This makes me think of Oliver North running for a senate seat, and abortion doctors murdered and eyes that watch but do not see. I think of the millions of eyes glued to TV screens watching soap operas and sitcoms while Ace and his friends are building up arsenals behind the walls of their clubhouse on Hamilton Avenue.

"Yeah," he told me, "we got a whole closet full of guns."

Maybe we are already doomed, but I don't want to be wearing an old flannel nightie and eating cupcakes when the enemy comes to find me, so I will increase my morning push-ups from twenty to fifty and with a magic marker write "No Surrender" on my labia to remind me.

Vision Quest

I used to consult the *I Ching* all the time. Should I call him, should I not call him? "Perseverance furthers" or "hasty action would not be wise," the book replied. The pages of my old journals are covered with those scratchy hexagrams, marks of my unquiet soul. Crouched in my room, throwing pennies on the floor, I asked the same questions again and again, buying time, biding time until my anger passed because my rage at the unfairness of life is so great I could kill. I was learning that there is no way you can make anyone love you and also that there are people who will love you no matter what you do, I brought my ex-husband to the house I shared with Peter and screwed him in our bed. When Peter found out his only comment was "I guess you had to get him out of your system." "Gradual Development" the *I Ching* said that day, "Progress."

I grew tired of the *I Ching*, Astrology, Tarot, all the gods of hocus-pocus, mumbo-jumbo, realized my friend, the astrologer Annette Planet, was the unhappiest person I ever had the sad fortune to know. When friends said they had to use the *I Ching* or throw the Runes, I heard myself say, "Can't you think for yourself?" One day I tossed my *I Ching* in the garbage, put on my magic red beret and went out into the street on a vision quest. The first thing I saw was a woman giving a man a blowjob in a silver Nissan Sentra.

I took up Yoga, learned to stand on my head, arch my back like a cat, coil like a cobra. The Yogis say that the body is a wishing stone. I found I could climb over mountains of anger doing breath of fire while seated in the lotus pose, but it was not enough. I used the credit card my parents gave me for emergencies to hop a plane for Barbados and, when a washed out old hippie soldier of fortune asked me to drop acid with him, I said yes. We sailed his boat to St. Thomas and there, in the Jewish cemetery at midnight, had intercourse on the grave of Isabella

Mariano Mendes, beloved daughter, mother, wife. He wanted to add me to his stable of three women, but I ran away, escaped with my life.

Back in New York, I have a miscarriage, drink coffee till my eyeballs sweat, start to write.

My Narcissism disgusts me and keeps me going at the same time. I read my poetry at Opens and learn that I am not the only one playing with a deck that has too many cards. I fall for a man who says that he will give me a baby, he gets cold feet, says that we are both too unstable, gives me an African violet instead. When I crush its leaves between my fingers, it bleeds a clear sap that smells like fresh-cut grass. I stay up all night trying to make the black shadows around me fade to purple. When people ask my astrological sign I lie and say I am a Scorpio if I want to appear sensual and exotic. I say I am a Libra if I want to be considered socially adept and well balanced. This little ruse works very well, but I am scared at how easily people accept these astrological categories as if the position of the stars was what it took to justify cruelty, avarice, and the failures of love.

I tell guys in bars that I am looking for a man with a heart in Aquarius, penis rising. They laugh, take a sip of beer, and look around the bar for another woman to talk to. Soon magazines begin to publish my poetry and I am invited to give readings. I have an affair with a bass player sixteen years younger than I. It starts out as a lark but the sex between us is so astounding I want to die with him. I know I'm out of control. I've stepped into a hole and am falling, but that does not stop me from baking him lasagnas, buying him silver jewelry. He is frightened of my intensity, does not want an aging wife, flees to New Mexico as many have done before him.

I go though menopause, have hot flashes, wet the bed at night while dreaming I am crawling through a tunnel towards a white light. Then I meet a college writing instructor, gorgeous, blue eyes with a chest like a stag, quite the catch. He has problems sustaining an erection and tells me it is my fault because I am a masochist and want to be hurt. Once I would have believed him, but now I throw him out. When I throw the *I Ching* it says, "Gradual development, progress...."

I no longer own an *I Ching,* but if I did, I wonder what it would say; "The Arousing, shock, thunder," or "Waiting, nourishment," or maybe "Work on what has been spoiled, decay."

Circe in the New Year

My father calls on the last day of the year to wish me a Happy New Year. He does not say maybe this year you'll get lucky and meet a rich guy, a nice guy or even a guy who can put up with you because my parents no longer ask about my love life. My brother has told me they are putting aside twenty dollars a week so I will not starve in my desolate old age. They have resigned themselves to my solitary condition, although I have not. They do not know how hot the hungry fires that rage between my legs are, nor would they understand why it is desire, not money or ambition, that rules me.

My father wants to know what's the good news, and I tell him the good news is there is no bad news, although I am lying. There is bad news in Haiti where the only maternity hospital in Port Au Prince has no sterilizer and more bad news on 149th Street in Jamaica Queens, where ten year olds carrying guns are selling crack cocaine; there the news is very bad indeed. I am lying about the news because ever since my father got his new plastic heart valve he does not want to discuss the woes of the world. If I mention the carnage in Chechnya he will say his chest hurts him. Since the operation, he lives in a ten-milligrams-of-Valium-twice-a-day world. He is afraid of getting excited; but today he is excited about something.

He tells me that a twenty-four-hour strip club named Circe's has opened up around the corner in what was Clyde's Chesapeake Crab House. The club is doing so much business that its parking lot is filled every day by eleven a.m. The patrons of Circe's are parking all around the block and taking up the available parking spots in the neighborhood.

"Who was Circe," my father wants to know, "some kind of Greek goddess?" I tell him she was a powerful witch who turned men into dogs and pigs. Then I say I think it is funny that the patrons of Circe's are hogging the parking spots. My father says there is nothing funny about it and that yesterday, when he and my mother where coming back from the Giant grocery store, they had to ride around for half an hour before they found a parking spot. The neighborhood association is going to picket Circe's starting tomorrow. He and my mother are going to join them.

I imagine my tiny, silver-haired mother in her Nikes walking a picket line chanting "Get the G-strings out of Silver Springs." I see my father, in his Baltimore Orioles cap, walking beside her, one hand clutching her elbow and the other nervously playing over his chest. Circe, the fox, has invaded Silver Springs and has got people up and clucking like chickens. I tell my father that a similar situation happened out on Long Island and the locals were able to close the club down. "I hope you have the same good luck," I say.

I wonder if the patrons of the club knew who Circe was and if the knowledge would deter them. I think not because Circe is the witch of uncontrollable desire, desire gone haywire. She is a vortex, a vacuum compactor, a Venus flytrap of a witch and none except the brain-dead or the living dead can resist the promises of her treacherous lips. In all of Greek mythology, only Odysseus was able to resist her and that was because Hermes gave him a magic potion to drink. Circe lives in the hands of men who batter women and in the women who cannot leave men who hurt them and the men who cannot leave women who hurt them.

I was in Circe's power when I spent the rent money on a silver bracelet for Skinny Fatts and when I called Bruno fourteen times in one morning until he disconnected his answering machine. Whenever I have tried to emulate Circe and work an enchantment to bind someone to me, it has backfired and then I was the one who became a pig or a dog. Now that I am a serious writer, there is so much I need to learn and so much I hope to say. I have no time to waste chasing my self-respect. I don't want to feel like my life is a Billy Holiday record ever again.

I have started to keep food in the house. I cook and feed myself. I painted my bedroom bone white to cover the heel marks my dirty feet left on the wall and eradicate the traces of last year's failed love affairs. I buy a vibrator and a book about tantric sex. The book says that tantric sex is the dimension of sex employed for consciousness expansion. This is what I want in the New Year, a love that will take me higher.

I take a little nap and go to Nina's annual New Year's Eve party. A twenty-two-year-old poet from Ireland named Sebastian, who has a voice like a babbling brook, says he wants to go home with me. His hands look so much like the soft hands of a child that I tell him no. Then I dance with a drummer from Trinidad who gets a huge erection while we are dancing to *Light My Fire*. I try to avoid the thick holiday log he is presenting me with by twisting my hips up and backward but I can still feel the tip of his insistent pole. He has a bland empty face and eyes in which nothing is happening. When he leans over and whispers into my ear, "I want to eat your pussy," his voice is harsh and low. "Thank you for the dance," I say. I tear myself out of his embrace only to have Nina grab me and pull me into a closet.

"I don't know what has happened to my life," she says. I tell her I feel the same way. Then she tells me she hasn't gotten laid once in the last year and if she does not get some loving soon she will go crazy. I tell her she should look for a relationship that will expand her consciousness and take her higher. I say she should stop obsessing about sex, although my dance with the drummer from Trinidad has left me so wet between the legs that in the confines of the closet I can smell myself. If this party is a harbinger of the New Year, I am afraid that Circe will haunt me everywhere.

I leave Nina's party soon after midnight. When I arrive home I put on Mozart's Horn Concerto, get out my new vibrator and hold a solitary little party to welcome the New Year. Then I fall into an exhausted sleep.

I wake around noon, take a shower and wash my hair. I have been invited to read that night with a hundred other poets at a New Year's Day reading at Cafe Nico. I practice reading and re-reading my poem, marking where to pause to take a breath and putting stars next to some lines to remind me to read them slowly.

Ursula comes over and we drive over the Brooklyn Bridge in my car to Café Nico, which is on Avenue A. She tells me about a housewarming party later that night in Williamsburg where there will be oysters and champagne. I say that after I read it might be fun to go over.

Café Nico is packed, there is free beer, plenty of good cheer. My poem in praise of the lumpy ungainly breast and undescended testicle goes over very well. Ursula and I stay and listen to the other poets. No one reads a poem about obsessive desire, which I take as a good sign, although several poets read poems about the possible relationships between Newt Gingrich and snakes, cobras, toads, pigs or other members of the animal kingdom. I am having such a good time that when Ursula suggests we leave for the party in Williamsburg I almost don't want to go, but my stomach is growling with hunger. The idea of a plate of fresh oysters is so appealing that I get my coat.

When we get to the party there are no oysters left. There is still some potato salad and deviled eggs. Ursula and I fill up plates. I see familiar faces, people I know from the Williamsburg arts scene. Everyone is talking about the closing of the much-loved Right Bank Bar. Bad management is what Otto says. Ursula says it was because there was never enough toilet paper in the bathrooms. I tell her that that is the sign of a great bar. Alexis is sure it was because Kevin, the owner, was putting the profits up his nose. We were all surprised the Right Bank closed so suddenly, maybe Kevin was sick of the grind or maybe Circe got him. Who can say why one venture succeeds or another fails? Why do some people mate early and well for life while others are always disappointed in romance? Why is the unexpected all you can expect? Why did my eyes suddenly meet the eyes of a tall man standing in the doorway of the room? He comes to sit next to me on the sofa, and tells me his name is Steven. He is a sculptor who works in leather and steel. He says he loves how I am dressed. I am glad, because I'm wearing my favorite orange and purple flowered velvet leggings, magic black cashmere sweater and my silver dancing shoes. I tell him I'm a poet and he says, "Even better." We talk some more and when he asks for my number I write it on my New Years poem and give it to him.

He calls the next day and tells me how much he liked the poem, he put it up on the wall in his studio. We have already had two dates. He likes to look into my eyes when he kisses me. I know the next time I see him we will go all the way. I can hardly wait. He is smart and has already caught me in a lie and refused to let me get away with it. I know he is the change I have been waiting for, which may be why today I woke up in the morning with a strong desire to get on a bus and run away to some small town in Connecticut and get a job in a K-Mart. Ursula says it is fear of intimacy, but I know it is Circe in the New Year coming after me. She is trying to change me into a scared little sparrow so I will fly away from this chance at happiness. I promise myself that I will vanquish Circe and hang in there, do what it takes, because I know that committing to another soul will be the most revolutionary stand I can make.

Courtship

I know Steven is serious. I know he has fallen for me big time. I knew it two weeks after we started seeing each other when he started to call me up every morning at eleven a.m. from his job to say, "Hello Angel, I miss you," even on the days he had just left my house three hours earlier. He keeps calling me Angel. He told me he had always wanted to call someone Angel and I was the one.

My reaction to this is mixed. On some days, I am a high-strung, gone old hippie babe; some days I'm a beauty. On other days I'm a vile witch, maybe I have swallowed so much acid that I never stropped tripping. Nonetheless, I've survived and miraculously become a late-blooming poet with a rising reputation for righteousness as well as an aging sex kitten with no patience for pretension. I love all language, even the so-called "blue words," the ones they bleep on TV, and especially the C word, the cunt word with that soft, groaning u, the wonderful u sound that is in udder or mother. I don't think there is any such thing as a dirty word.

There is plenty of dirt under my bed, however, as I'd rather do Yoga than clean my house. I have no patience for intellectuals, although I read at least five books a week. I envy, lust for and covet four of my friends' husbands, which makes me guilty of three of the seven deadly sins. I still have trouble controlling my angry outbursts. I'm quite capable of cruelty, particularly when someone else's weakness reminds of my own. I don't want to be put up on a pedestal. I don't want to be worshipped and I'm certainly no angel, far from it. I want to be accepted for who and what I am, with my crooked teeth and stretch marks.

I try to tell this to Steven when we are lying on my bed, our heads on one pillow. I can still taste his salt on my mouth. "But Angel," he says, "I do accept you as you are. You are my angel." I find myself thinking maybe I should fuck his best friend Gary, who is very flirtations with me. Then I could tell Steven about it and see if he still thinks I am his angel. I hate myself for thinking like this.

"I am not just your angel," I tell Steven, "I'm also my own devil as well as my own worst enemy and you better start listening to what I'm saying." Then I storm off to the bathroom and take a cold shower.

Recently, when he was visiting, he started to fold and put away the clothes I'd left on the floor. "Stop it," I told him, "If I want to leave my things in a mess, it's my business. Stop acting like my mother."

He looked at me like I had slapped him, "But, Angel," he told me, "I want to take care of you."He looked so sweet and sad, standing there, holding my old, worn, red Che Guevera t-shirt in his hand that I took pity on him.

"If you want to take care of me, why don't you come over here and kiss me?" I said. He did and then we spent a very nice hour in my bed.

Still, no matter what he says, he doesn't accept me for who I am. When he is visiting and he notices that I have left the cap off the toothpaste, which I do all the time, he puts it back on. He tries to interfere with my costume choices. Last Saturday evening, when he picked me up to go to Gary's birthday party, I answered the door wearing my long, red velvet sheath dress, an Isaye Miyaki dress that I was so lucky to find in the Salvation Army for$9.99. His face fell when he saw me.

"Why don't you wear that short pink dress you wore to Zeta's opening?" he asked. "I like how it shows off your legs."

"But Steven," I told him, "I love this dress, it's so elegant. Besides I don't want to change, I'm all ready to go." He shook his head but he didn't say anything else. We went to the party with me wearing the Isaye Miyaki dress.

At the party, after a couple of glasses of wine, I managed to drop a chip loaded with babaganoosh on my dress, leaving a big, oily stain. He ran to get a wet cloth and wipe it off. My first thought was that he was so quick to get that cloth because he is embarrassed at having a slob for a girlfriend. I told myself that was crazy thinking, he was only trying to be nice to me. "There, there," he said, as he finished the task, "I wouldn't want to ruin your elegant dress. It looks good as new, even though it is second-hand, isn't it?" There was an edge to his voice and I didn't like the little comment. Could it be my old tried and true fear of intimacy that was making me so critical of him, than again, maybe I wasn't nit picking, maybe he really is a nit?

Every time he comes over he brings me two gallons of bottled water and two big rolls of toilet paper. At first I thought these were cute courtship gifts, but now I have thirty-two rolls of toilet paper in the cabinet under my bathroom sink, and sixteen gallons of bottled water in my clothes closet. If I'm still asleep when he wakes up, he will get up and sweep the floor, neaten up the bedroom. I don't want a maid. I want a man who wakes me up by kissing my tits.

Sometimes we spend the night in the loft bed in his studio and the last thing I want to do in the morning if he is still sleeping beside me is to get up and sweep his floor. I want to just lie beside him and smell him. Maybe I am the romantic in the relationship and he is the practical one, maybe that's a good balance. I don't know. Time will tell. Right now I know I like his smell so much that I will let him court me and see where it goes.

Frogs

Steven and I are making love when he suddenly says, "Angel, you're bleeding." This is suspicious because I am past menopause and have not had a period in three years.

Sitting in the gynecologist's office a few days later, I read in the *Scientific American* that frogs are vanishing from the earth. Ultra violet radiation is breaking through the ozone layer, killing the eggs frogs lay in shallow ponds; the natural habitats of frogs have been destroyed by the cutting down of forests, plus the French eat three to four metric tons of frogs' legs a year. If only the frogs, such ancient creatures of myth and magic, were vanishing because they were blessed with love and turning into princes and princesses, but it is no longer the age of fairy tales. I am simultaneously disgusted and frightened by the rape of the earth, the gluttony of the French and my powerlessness to control the inner workings of my own body.

The gynecologist positions my feet in the stirrups, asks me to slide down the examining table so he can get the best possible view. Why have I not noticed before, in all the years I have been coming to see him, that with his bald head and big, protruding eyes he looks like a frog? His hand, as he pushes my knees wider apart, is moist and clammy. He inserts the speculum.

It is so cold that shivers run up and down my spine and I tense up. "Relax, relax," the gynecologist peeps and chirps, "I'm not going to hurt you," he says and he does not. He puts on a pair of magnifying glasses with double lenses. He peers inside, palpates my belly, my uterus, says that everything appears normal. He suggests a pelvic sonogram, further tests. This suggestion is what hurts. I have no medical insurance, no money, am using my rent money to pay for this office visit.

I tell him this and he suggests a clinic where they will do the sonogram for only $125. But that is still pie in the sky to me. Then, pointing to two black and blue marks on the inside of my upper thighs, the gynecologist gently asks me if my boyfriend and I are into rough sex. I have not even noticed these marks and wonder if Steven made them by pressing down with his palms, urging me to open to him. If rough sex means that we are impervious to everything but our need for each other when we are doing it, than yes, we are into rough sex, but I do not wish to discuss my love life with the gynecologist, benevolent frog though he may be. I tell him not especially.

Out in the street I stuff the paper with the address of the clinic that will give me the pelvic sonogram I know I cannot afford deep into the pocket of my old black jeans and head for the subway. I wonder if I was bleeding because I use blue toilet paper or if the bleeding was caused by environmental pollutants or if ultra violet radiation is burning holes in my veins or in my brain.

At the entrance to the subway an old woman with a Medusa's head of ratty hair lurches into me, thrusting out a grimy paper cup. "Please miss," she says, her spittle spraying my face. I recoil, perhaps too late, has she given me tuberculosis, pneumonia? I dash down the stairs and score a seat on the Lexington Avenue #4 Downtown. The big man seated next to me wearing army fatigues is breathing hard, clutching a large Duane-Reade bag between his knees. It could hold a pipe bomb, maybe I should move to the next car, but I stay where I am, fear makes me rigid. It is no longer possible for me to protect the boundaries of my own body, if it ever was, and no one is safe. I feel like a frog speared on a stick. I wonder if the frogs know they are faced with extinction. I wonder how they think, what they know. I know I have not been happy of late and once home I get out of my coat and go to the phone to call Steven but something stops me.

I sit down on the bed and realize that I am very tired. I lie down, curl up in the fetal position and, crossing my arms on my chest, rock myself from side to side. Steven will not say he loves me. If I ask him if he does, he says, "What's your take on that?" yet whenever he seems to need assurance, I give it to him. My brother, who has met him, says, "It's obvious he is wild about you. A lot of men have trouble saying "I love you" straight out, so why rag Steven about it?"

"It's a small thing," my brother says, but somehow it's not a small thing. Maybe I am stitched together by insecurities or maybe I am like my mother, always needing to be in control.

Steven and I are developing other problems; he has lost his job, through no fault of his own.

He had nothing put away, has borrowed to the max from his friends and now, when he comes over, he says, he hates to ask but could I spare a five? A ten? I have so little but how can I refuse him? I smile and say, sweetheart, if the situation was reversed I know you would float me a little loan. I go to my purse, but these little loans are beginning to add up and lately we are both on the defensive. I learned a long time ago that love is not a panacea, but I am beginning to feel as though I have opened up Pandora's Box.

The things I don't want to see about myself, Steven sees and he is not shy about pointing them out. He wants to know why I am not looking harder for an agent to help me sell my book, why my toilet bowl is filthy, why I eat so much sugar that it is a miracle I do not have diabetes? I tell him that I don't want to hear it, that I want unconditional love just like I am giving him and that I love him even if he is a chain smoker. As soon as he leaves I rush to throw open the windows and air out the room. Actually, I am more dismayed by how much grass he smokes. He says it helps him keep calm. I think the opposite, that smoking grass makes him even more high-strung.

I wonder if what we are building together is a house of cards, a loony bin, a portable pissoir and why, of all the 5.7 billion people on the planet, I hooked up with this one. Only time will tell, love is a riddle, love is a spell, love is a bell that's ringing me and I don't like it.

I fantasize about running away, but where would I go, to sleep with the hobos under the Boardwalk in Coney Island? Maybe I can join the frogs hopping through moist shady woods and lolling about in lagoons, but I would not be happy there, far from my books, my typewriter, my telephone. It occurs to me that I don't know much about frogs except that they are not always green and that the croaking of the frogs, the frog chorus, is a mating song the male frogs have been singing to the female frogs since before the time of the dinosaurs. I lie in my bed between waking and sleeping, rocking myself, thinking of Steven and me. Despite all the evidence to the contrary, there is an idea of the union of love, love that can save the world. It is what the frogs know, singing through millennia, it is the courtship song that opens into all creation; if the frogs become extinct, we are all lost, maybe we are lost already.

I stay in bed hugging myself while the day falls away into darkness. I am roused by the phone. It is Steven calling to say he wants to come right over.

"Don't you want to hear what the doctor had to say?" I ask him.

"It can wait," he tells me. I am miffed. Doesn't he care? Forty minutes later I let him in the door, he is carrying a bottle of red Chianti wine just like he did the first night he came to see me. He says his boss called him, wants him back on the job. I tell him that's great, and then tell him what the doctor had to say about the pelvic sonogram. Steven says, "No problem, Angel, I can cover it," and quick as a frog I leap into his arms.

Butterflies

Steven wants us to get married, but I don't want to. I tell him that I don't believe in marriage. From what I've seen, marriage is too often the death of hope, and at its very best it is an uneasy series of compromises. I tell Steven I want only him, but I love him too much to marry him.

Marriage is an outmoded convention, I tell him, after all fifty percent of all first marriages end in divorce and seventy-five percent of all second marriages do the same.

I sit on Steven's lap, whisper I love him, but then I tell him that I am an anarchist and don't need the state to legitimize how I feel. He picks me up off his lap and sets me down on my white wicker rocking chair, goes to the refrigerator, gets out a beer, and sits back in the big armchair. He says he always wanted a wife. It took him years to find me and I am the one. He says relationships based solely on personal inclination flounder. He wants to be with me for the rest of his life, he says he is an old-fashioned kind of guy. I tell him I find his old-fashioned attitude incongruous in a man who designs leather underwear, leather masks, and sex toys for a living. He says he does not see why.

I laugh; he is hurt. We quarrel. He calls me flaky; I call him insecure. We get out the bottle of scotch we keep in the cabinet over the sink to referee arguments and soon we are wrestling in the matrimonial position on the floor. This is one kind of matrimony I don't mind. Our match ends in a draw, but he won't let it go.

He keeps bringing up the subject. Over morning coffee he wants to know what I'm afraid of. Shopping for vegetables in the supermarket, when I don't want to try kohlrabi, he wants to know why I'm so fearful of trying new things. I feel like I am under siege. I start to take long walks by myself, binge eat on pizza and ice cream. I stop doing yoga, stop flossing my teeth. If I gain ten pounds and develop dog breath, maybe he will leave — but I know if he leaves I will be devastated.

When I was eighteen I married the first guy I did it with and that was a disaster. I threw my wedding ring in a sewer on Ocean Parkway on a rainy spring day and promised myself I would not marry again. When I think of myself in the married state, butterflies invade my stomach, colonize, multiply, storm my esophagus, fly up my windpipe, lodge in my throat, choke me.

One night, with Steven sleeping beside me, I have the butterfly dream. In the dream, my father, not the bald, scrawny old man he is now, but my young, virile father with his black, wavy hair and strong swimmer's thighs is wearing a pair of tight, white B.V.D.'s and chasing me through a country field waving a big butterfly net. I am running as fast as I can, but he is gaining. "I've got you now," he cries, dropping the net over my head. The mesh cuts into my face and my nose, stuffs my mouth. I do not have to be Sigmund Freud to figure out what this dream means; I have been having it on and off since I was five years old. It started after the summer my mother and I spent in a bungalow colony in the Catskills. My father and the other men whose families were vacationing there came up from New York to spend the weekends. During this summer my father took up catching butterflies. He bounded around in the meadows, and when he caught a specimen he would put it in a glass jar he carried with him in his knapsack. In the evenings, he would mount the beautiful, now-dead creatures in a special book he had, securing them with special pins he had for that purpose. Also, during this summer, my parents started yelling at each other. They fought about my mother's compulsions for cleaning and control, and my father's gambling.

My mother programmed me well: I always have to fight the desire to tell other people what to do. Steven is not my father; I am not my mother, but maybe if I marry the need to control she imprinted in me will be so overwhelming that I won't be able to stop myself. Steven will get sick of fighting it, look elsewhere for support and encouragement, and my sorry family history will repeat itself.

That history, as well as my own early flop of a marriage, made me eschew marriage and choose the adventurer's life. One full-moon night, high on acid out in the Provincetown dunes, Judy Mazzola and I tasted each other's menstrual blood and vowed to pursue only the best men and the best drugs for the rest of our lives. For the last fifteen years she has been married to an accountant in Albuquerque and she has given birth to three sons. In the photo of her family that she sends me each Christmas I see a plump, pleasant matron with Dolly Parton hair. I can find no trace at all of the wild, tough beauty who shared Finn Connor with me on so many nights through one summer. We used to flip a coin to see who would go first. If I marry, I fear I will loose my wildness, my waistline, my wanderlust.

I give a poetry reading with Danny Matthew, a dear friend who has been married for ten years. After the reading, we are drinking gin and tonics at Milano's and I pommel him with my anti-marriage diatribe. He says that he is mostly happy and that he knows he would be much crazier without Simone and the boys. I tell him I am afraid of loosing my edge. He answers me immediately with no hesitation. "You will, but you won't know until after you try whether that will help or hurt you as a writer." I tell him, "Thanks a lot," Later that night, I tell Steven I am not ready yet and it may be years until I am.

"How many years?" Steven wants to know. "If you are not ready at fifty-one, when will you be ready, when you are eighty-five?" He says he is going to spend the night in his studio and storms out the door. Immediately, I miss him and think what a fool I am, maybe he won't come back. If he doesn't come back I will be free again, free as a butterfly. I can spend the rest of my life flying around, having casual sex, eating nectar out of flowers. What a bore.

I go lie down in bed. I have not changed the sheets for a week and Steven's smell, the Florida water he uses for cologne mixed with spicy sweat smells, is all around me. I ask myself what I am ready for, a lobotomy, a double-headed dildo?

I know that there is no more preposterous, radical or courageous statement I can make, especially given my record of dismal failure in affairs of the heart, than to marry a man I have known for six months, who is thirteen years my junior, who keeps telling me I look like Jean Harlow and who says he wants to be buried with me. Presented with a long shot like this, an adventurer like myself has no choice but to go for it.

I get out of bed, go to the phone and dial Steven's studio. I let the phone ring ten times but he does not pick up, I walk around the apartment, bounce off the walls for an hour, try again with no success. Where can he be? His studio is only six blocks away. I finish the bottle of Scotch, polish off three stale English muffins that have been sitting in the refrigerator since Memorial Day. I light the blue candle that's on the kitchen table as a memorial to my lost love. If I can only see him again, I will do anything to keep him; do his laundry, bake him marble cakes, clean out his rectum twice daily with my tongue.

I try calling again but no one picks up. First light is breaking through the window. The deli on the corner is opening, so I decide to get a cup of their acrid coffee to pick me up. I step out in the hall. As I am locking my door I glance out the hall window and am astonished to see two large feet shod in a pair of familiar black Doc Martens. At first I think I am hallucinating, but I step over to the window and see that the feet are connected to Steven's long legs. He is sleeping on the fire escape, curled up in the fetal position, and the sight of him is so dear that I begin to cry. He has made a pillow of his sweatshirt and, from where I am standing, I can see the tattoo of a rising sun he has on his right forearm. I climb out on the fire escape and curl up beside him. I make no effort to wake him but a few minutes later when he opens his eyes I tell him I have changed my mind. I want to marry him.

"You won't be sorry," he says, and then we climb off the fire escape, go inside, and lie down on the bed. We hold each other, my arms around his back, his hands on my ass. I feel as if I have stepped over the edge of the world into the unknown. I hope our life together will be as rich and full of color as a field of butterflies, but who knows?

Ball and Chain

Steven and I got married, which surprised everyone, since my views on marriage are well-known. More than one of my friends and drinking buddies has expressed astonishment, and as one colleague put it, "You, of all people, why?"

The truth is that I don't know, I can offer no explanations or justification. The answer does not lie inside the lonely garden between my thighs or printed inside a Valentine. The story of a Welsh painter I once picked up in Puffy's floats into mind. He told me nothing got him going like a pair of scanty panties made of satin or lace and then he asked me if I had pretty knickers on. Because I wanted to ball him I lied and said yeah even though I had on an old stretched-out white cotton pair. The discovery of my deception did not prevent him from giving me a rigorous reaming and then he got out of my bed and pulled a package of Newport Lights and a narrow gold band out of his inside jacket pocket. He slid the gold band on the third finger of his left hand and said, "I couldn't penetrate my wife, so I married her. I still can't penetrate her; but we're much happier now." I was too aghast to ask him what he meant by "penetrate." Did he mean it in the sense of "to enter", or did he mean it in the sense of "to understand"? Did I marry Steven because I couldn't understand him and didn't know what else to do? I cannot understand why, in spite of how much we love each other, it is so hard for us to communicate. Maybe I married him because it was either leave him or marry him and I don't want to leave him. Maybe I married him because of guys like the Welsh painter.

For so many years I walked around wearing a T-shirt that said Unclaimed; now that I am married, I still feel isolated and deranged. Marrying him has not made me believe in eternal life or the transmigration of souls, nor has it mended the holes in my old black cashmere sweater or made me a better person. I still imagine that the group of people standing in the corner by the food table at a party is laughing at me. I still don't give change to homeless people. I am still convinced that I am being constantly lied to and betrayed by everyone. It is only when I'm around Steven that I don't feel that way.

Around him, I want to drink sparkling wine and dance the hoochie-coochie nude except for a pair of red high-heeled shoes. He likes it when I dance before him nude; he likes how my small, pendulous breasts bob and sway; maybe that's part of the why I married him. For a marriage gift I gave him a half-dead poinsettia plant that I found in the street on New Year's Day three days after our nuptials at City Hall; he gave me a dozen deep pink roses, which he bought with his last twenty dollars. I don't know what, if anything, this says about the balance of power in our lives. Sometimes our inability to communicate makes me so crazy that I feel as dangerous as a crack addict with a switchblade knife and other times, like when he happens to knock on my writing room door to bring me a coffee, I feel as if I've strayed into an earthly paradise.

Two days before the ceremony we went to City Hall to get the license, which cost thirty dollars. No blood test was required, but you had to wait at least twenty-four hours after you got the license to marry. We were so broke that when we got home we had to roll pennies to scrape together the twenty-five-dollar fee we needed for the marriage ceremony.

The morning of our wedding day was bitter cold, yet we walked over the Brooklyn Bridge to City Hall holding hands. We met our witness, my oldest and dearest friend, Harriet, outside the chapel. To transform myself into a beautiful bride, I had taken the three Valium hidden in a sock in my underwear drawer since February 1993. They had been given to me by another juror when I was on a jury in a rape case. I wore a blouse that my mother had made from a silk parachute my father used when he parachuted into Normandy in 1944 and my favorite pair of black jeans. Harriet took her gold hoop earrings out of her ears and gave them to me to wear for luck. Waiting for our names to be called in the waiting room outside the chapel with a dozen or so other couples and their witnesses, I wondered if I will actually be able to swear to love, honor and obey Steven till death do us part, but once inside the chapel I discover that these words are not even mentioned. When the Justice of the Peace, a hip-looking woman wearing John Lennon glasses, asks me if I take Steven to be my husband, I manage to sputter out an "I do," but when she says does anyone here know of a reason why this marriage should not take place I want to shout out, "Yes, I do, I'm too wild, too crazy to marry!" but I am so zonked on Valium and the heebie-jeebies that I cannot speak, so the justice of the peace pronounces us man and wife and I enter the problematic, many-petaled state of illusion that is matrimony.

After the ceremony Harriet takes us out for a wedding breakfast at a glorified diner owned by a former Miss Subways on lower Broadway. Harriet has a BLT, I have two pieces of cherry cheesecake, and Steven has eggs and steak. Sitting between two people who love me, eating cheesecake in the muted light of the diner under the pictures of old Miss Subways, many of whom must now be dead, I experience a curious, new feeling of serenity and peace that I decide must be married bliss.

This feeling lasts until Steven and I get home to find that someone has left open the refrigerator door and there is water all over the floor. Steven says that I must have left the door open because I have done it before, and I say, defensively, "So what? If there is water on the floor, I'll mop it up." As I get the mop, he changes his clothes because he has to go out to Astoria to check out a job. He kisses me a little peck of a kiss and leaves. I mop the floor and then call my family to tell them that I am married.

My mother answers and when I tell her my news she says congratulations and then she wants to know how I spell my new last name. When I tell her that I've kept my old name she sounds perplexed. "But how shall I tell the relatives to make out the wedding-present checks?"she asks. I want to tell her to hold off for at least two years in case the marriage is an early failure. I don't want to have to return the money and I wonder what people do in such cases; then I tell my mother to have the checks made out to me. There is a pause on the other end of the phone and my mother, who has, over the last few years, made a determined effort to be more accepting of me, says, "Well, I guess you know what you're doing, dear, but aren't Steven's feelings hurt because you haven't taken his name?"

"Oh, he doesn't care, Ma," I tell her and I say good-bye and get off the phone. But he does care. He asked me to take his name and I said no. He also cares that my clothes make big haystack piles on the floor until I'm ready to put them away, just as I care that he smokes so much reefer, yet we have managed to become an official pair. Sometimes we act too much like Lucy and Ricky for comfort's sake, but perhaps in time we will mellow out and come to be more like George and Gracie.

Our marriage is a month old and it hasn't been easy. Sometimes I see us as if we are in a cartoon, leaping towards each other. I am jumping off a small ice floe marked "solitary narcissism" to join him on a larger one marked "mutual despair" but so far, like a river surrounding us, the love is still there.

Cosmic Debris

All day long, as I sit at my typewriter, drink tea, feed the cat, pass gas, talk on the telephone, I feel as if an invisible cord connects me to Steven. I know his whereabouts. He is working a job on Fifty-Seventh Street and Tenth Avenue. He is also somehow inside of me and connected to me. If this is what bonding means, I don't like it. I can sense how hard, how painful it would be to tear the cord out and break free. Even though the invisible cord is made from hope, memory and ectoplasmic light, I can feel how strong it is. As long as it stretches between us, everything I do affects him and everything he does affects me. I really have to watch my ass: no flirting with the young James Stewart behind the counter in the video store; no telling lies; no saying I am going to spend the day writing and then slinking off to Domsey's in search for a fringed suede jacket that will keep me forever young.

I wish I could relax into this marriage, kind of go with the flow, but I have spent so many years staying high by frantically bouncing off the walls that I don't know how to take it slow. Also, as I grow older, I feel like a tornado of confused feelings, hurtling through time, faster and faster, while the end of the world is gaping before me like a pit. I open the window to let in some fresh air, but remember too late that this is New York and there is none left. A gray-black cloud wafts in smelling of damp newspapers and dried urine, burned cigarettes and soon specks of cosmic debris are covering the tables, chairs, books. The ashes of lost souls are falling on the bed and sticking to the top sheet. I leap up, close the window, but it is as if the sooty dust is everywhere. I wet a sponge, take up a roll of paper towels. The going is slow but I persevere and soon the table is clear of dust. I go to the shelves, take down each book, wipe it, put it back.

When I get to my photo album, two pictures fall to the floor. I pick one up. It is a picture of my first husband, Eddie Zimmer, his dark hair slicked back into a D.A. He is grinning insolently into the camera. I have long ago stopped caring where he is as long as he is far away from me. After he screwed me he used to say, "If only you were prettier, I could go longer." I tear this picture up, throw it in the garbage.

I think about how, when we are not fighting, Steven likes to call me Angel. I once asked him if he called all his girlfriends Angel, much as Elvis called all his women Hon. Steven said, "No, just you, I always wanted to call someone Angel, and it's you." Lately, though he has not been calling me "Angel" very much. I pick the second picture up from the floor. The face of my Grandpa Jack at his eightieth birthday party shines out. In one hand he is holding what I know to be a glass filled with Johnny Walker Black Label because that was his only drink. The other hand is proudly on the shoulder of my Grandma Fanny. They were married happily for fifty-five years and died a month apart. I wish Grandpa Jack would materialize out of the cosmic debris and tell me the secret of a happy marriage.

Ingrid Bergman said that a bad memory helps, but than she didn't have much married luck. Maybe you just have to keep working at it. Steven says it should not be work, it should come naturally, but I don't know what, if anything, is natural in the Universe anymore. When I was four years old, Grandpa Jack taught me to tie my shoelaces into neat little bows so I could walk away from my too-doting mother with her frequent admonitions: "don't do this" and "no-no-no." He also told me that when we humans walk down the street, we are preceded by hordes of angels singing, "Make way, make way for the image of God." I take this picture of my grandparents and tuck it into the frame of the mirror that hangs over our bed. Perhaps they will inspire us, but Steven may think we do not need any inspiration. I promise myself I will be cool if he wants to take the picture down, but since I am always making fusses over small things like his leaving the toilet seat up, I wonder if I will be able to keep this promise. The phone rings and it is my friend Lynn who tells me that her husband, Mark, has lost his job and the medical insurance that goes along with it.

They are desperately trying to get him some of the new HIV Protease inhibitor that is saving lives. She says he is too ill to take the subway; they don't have money for a taxi. Am I free to drive them to an interview for a new research program that will, if he is accepted, provide him with the drug? While she is talking I feel wretched about my ingrown pettiness and guilty about Steven's and my good health. He is not perfect, but he is not dying either. What would I do if he were? I tell Lynn that I will pick them up in an hour, then hurriedly put on my coat, gather my driver's license, registration, keys, and run out the door and into the car before the cosmic debris swallows me.

Fighting the Tide

Steven and I are in the back seat of my parents Toyota Camry in a parking lot in Silver Springs, Maryland. We have just come out of a terrible, overpriced Italian restaurant called Lido's where the pasta tastes like cardboard. My father puts the key in the ignition but before he turns it, he looks at my mother. With a tenderness so palpable I hear violins, he says, "How are you doing, kid?" My mother, whose arthritis has recently spread to her spine, shakes her head, "not so good," she sighs. She adjusts the collar of her favorite coral silk blouse as if this will make her feel better. Maybe it does, because she moves closer to my father, rests her head on his shoulder.

I flash back to a family outing to Brighton Beach sometime in the late 1950s. My mother is wearing a two-piece swimsuit that's coral, one of her favorite colors. She and I have just come out of the water, we approach the blanket, reach down for our towels. My father looks up from the racing form he has been reading and says to me with obvious pride. "Look at your mother. You two could be twins. She looks like a kid."

My mother does not look like a kid anymore; her face is cross-hatched with lines. She has lost a lot of weight and her clothes all look outsized. Twice during this visit she has forgotten my name and called me "Mildred" after her dead sister.

When we get back to my brother's house, where Steven and I are staying, my brother and mother start talking in the kitchen and Steven goes to the backyard with my six-year-old niece and three-year-old nephew to play catch. My father takes me aside and leads me down to the basement recreation room where we sit on the couch across from the cabinet holding my brother's collection of antique vases. Once, when we were smoking hashish my brother told me he collected vases because they reminded him of vaginas.

"Look at your mother," he says, "she looks like an old lady. She falls asleep in front of the TV every night. Last night she fell asleep in the middle of *NYPD Blue,* and it's her favorite show." He then goes on to tell me that, after fifty years of nagging him about the water he leaves on the bathroom floor when he showers, she no longer mentions it. She has recently abandoned her daily ritual of dusting every surface in the house. He says he is very worried about her.

"Well, she is seventy-eight. No one can fight the tide," I add, which is what my friend Lynn's husband, Mark, said to her last week from his hospital bed, a day before he died from HIV/AIDS. I tell my father I am worried about my mother too, then we both sit staring at my brother's collection of vases, which remind me of Georgia O'Keefe's flowering pudendas and my mother's vanished beauty and the tiny blue veins that are flowering on my thighs like tiny forget-me-nots. I don't want my mother to die, I don't want to die and a terrified voice inside me cries out into the black merciless void NO, NO, NO, NO.

My father speaks and changes the subject; he says he likes Steven so much.

"Tell me," he asks, leaning closer, "Does Steven mind that you are thirteen years older than he? Does he even know?" He is gazing at me earnestly, sincerely, like a talk show host who wants me to confide in him. He apparently has no idea that he has said anything hurtful or stupid.

"No, he doesn't mind," I yell.

"No need to get excited," my father says, "As long as you two are happy."

I start to feel delirious. I think about how I try to hide the lines that are forming around my mouth under a coat of powder and how I do Yoga and fifty push-ups a day in an attempt to say lithe and slim. Lately, a few times, when Steven and I have been talking at a party, I have noticed his gaze stray to other women, all of whom looked younger than me. Also, we are fighting more lately, petty quarrels about ridiculous things like why I keep forgetting to put the cap back on the tube of toothpaste. I tell him to put the cap back on if it bothers him or to get his own tube of toothpaste. He tells me that when I leave the cap off it attracts bugs. I tell him the only bugs around are in his head. He storms out of the house, slamming the door behind him. I go to bed and masturbate, choosing to imagine one of my old lovers, Dickie O., but still it is Steven's face I see as I am working my fingers between my legs.

My father starts to talk about the expensive convalescent and hospice care insurance policies he and my mother have taken out so that they will not be a burden to my brother and me. I have heard about this so often that I feel like I am going to burst into tears but manage to control myself by staring at a large white vase that opens out purple on top like the petals of an orchid.

The next day Steven and I head home in our battered 1984 Chevrolet, an outer space cowboy from California and his sad-eyed poet lady from Brooklyn. I don't have much to say. Visiting my family always makes me crazy, makes me unravel at the seams.

"You're so quiet. Worried about your mom?" Steven asks. I say yes and then he suggests lunch at the next rest stop. We drive up the Jersey Turnpike to the rest stop listening to Iggy Pop singing "I Wanna Be Your Dog."

As we walk though the lobby of the rest area building, I only see white faces. Most of the men are wearing baseball caps and windbreakers; most of the women are wearing jeans and hoodies. Steven's waist-length blond hair attracts some attention.

Seated in a turquoise blue booth in the Howard Johnson's we read the menus printed on the placemat. I tell Steven I will have a spinach salad, he opts for the rib steak. The waitress is a pert redheaded vixen in a blue-and-white checked uniform. She swings her hips back and forth like a metronome as she approaches. She gives Steven a radiant smile.

"Good afternoon," she says. "What can I get you?"

"I'll have a Guinness," he answers, "and the rib steak medium rare," but she cuts in before he can give my order. "And for your mother?" she asks grinning at him.

Steven does not miss a beat, "My wife," he says with a slightly louder emphasis on the word "wife," "will have a glass of white wine and the spinach salad."

The waitress snickers. "I'm sorry," she says, still grinning. Under Steven's now steely gaze she writes our order down and goes to place it. Cunt, douche bag, dildo, I call silently to her retreating back. These are words that are very dear to me, yet somehow, when I am hurt, I cannot stop myself from using these words as curse words. Steven takes my hand, squeezes it. I bite my tongue to keep from asking him if I look old enough to be his mother.

The Wheel

It is Monday, September 25th, Rosh Hashanah, the first day of the Jewish New Year, and I am doing yoga on my kitchen floor. The yogis say the body is a wishing stone. As I bend and stretch and breathe I feel so good, so happy in my body that I wish I could live forever.

Today, all over the world, Jews are tossing bread into oceans, rivers, lakes in the ceremony of Tashlich, a symbolic casting out of their sins. I say I do not believe in this ceremony.

I say sometimes I believe in a God or Gods, sometimes I believe only chaos is God, but nonetheless I was raised to be an observant Jew. While I may call myself agnostic, here I am on this high holy day thinking about my sins and working out on my Yoga mat, which is the now-worn pink blanket my grandmother gave me when I was five. I am wearing my yoga outfit, which is my red Harley Davidson tee shirt and an old pair of pink panties with loose elastic at the waist and a few holes above the crotch. I know my sins are plenty and today I feel a need to at least identify them and dive under the layers of arrogance, fear and denial that have invaded my head like a virus. I want to pull them up, cast my sins out into the light.

I lie flat on my back, bend my knees, and place my arms behind my shoulders. Taking a deep breath, I push upwards so the apex of my body, my navel, is pointing to the ceiling. This is the wheel pose, one of my favorites. I meditate on my sins. The first one that floats into my mind is gluttony. I am greedy about and for so many things. I can never get enough kisses, orgasms, poetry. I make snap judgments of people based on imagined insults, I don't stop to ask what they meant by this or that comment, maybe they weren't even thinking about me at all, maybe they were just having a bad day. I am not forgiving, I don't give second chances. I am wasteful and careless with money. I usc too much toilet paper, butter my bread on both sides, I waste time, much too much time. I lie cozy in bed for hours reading trashy novels when I should be washing the dishes, the floors, the dust out of my head.

I've wasted months, even years, staying in relationships when I already knew they were over. There was nothing more to learn and lingering would only be throwing effort after foolishness. Yet, I stayed.

I wonder if I eventually will do this with Steven. For the past few weeks, we have not been communicating well at all. Before he moved in I thought his habit of smoking a joint in bed first thing in the morning was an occasional thing. Now I know that he never gets up to start the day unless he is stoned first. When I ask him why, he says he is medicating himself like this, he tells me he is having a lot of stress on the job. He works for a company building sets for TV shows and commercials. He says he's afraid he'll loose his temper, mouth off and get fired. He tells me the grass calms him down. Then he adds that I don't spend enough time with him, that I'm always writing or doing yoga. I tell him meditation might help him more than grass and he knew how much writing and doing yoga meant to me before he married me. In response, he grabs his stash out of his dresser drawer and then he storms out the door.

My legs and arms are beginning to ache, but I concentrate on the rhythm of my breathing and stay in the pose. The yogis say serenity can be achieved by breathing slowly, that fast-breathing creatures have excitable temperaments and live short lives. The long-living tortoise only breathes three times a minute. I pretend I am placid and open my mind, but then my sins come buzzing into my head like a plague of flies. I bully my friends. I decide I want to go to a certain restaurant or movie and nothing else will do. If they don't agree I sulk until the give in to me. I am often too flip and not compassionate. When June came to talk to me about Kevin's drinking, I told her to drop him, that he wasn't worth her time, brusquely dismissing their seventeen years together, their two children.

The ache in my legs and arms has spread all the way up my spine, through my shoulders. I glance at the clock, only three minutes left. I'm going to make it! Suddenly, Steven bursts through the door, home from work two hours early.

"Hi Angel!" he calls out. He flashes me a big smile and then he notices me upside down on the floor in my panties and tee shirt. "Wow, what a view," he says. I'm going to take off my pants and hop on top of you."

This totally breaks my concentration and I collapse into a sprawl.

"This is my yoga time," I tell him, more than a little sharply. "You know how important it is to me."

His eyes flash blue lightning and he stops smiling. "Okay," he says, "I'll go to visit Jack next door and smoke the special pot with him that I just brought home to smoke with you."

"Fine with me," I tell him and he goes out, slamming the door.

I push up into the wheel again, try to calm my breathing without much success. Now I feel guilty about rejecting him, but yoga is the backbone of my life. It helps me find my strength. Besides, I don't want to smoke grass now in the middle of the day, especially this High Holy Day. Than again, maybe I am not flexible enough, maybe I am too set in my ways, maybe I just do not have the stamina for a long-term relationship but then I remind myself I do yoga to increase stamina. I check the clock once more and decide to stretch those last three minutes to five.

I breathe slower and slower and I can feel my spine relaxing, letting go. My sex releases like a lotus unfolding and my head droops back like a flower reclining on a stem. My friend Ursula, who makes sculptures out of flowers, says it is not easy to share your life with another. She ought to know ñ she was married for twenty years. I wonder why it has to be like that. Maybe Steven is not the right one after all, but he is the one I chose after many others wanted to husband me. I think of how I lied to him right at the start and of the other lies I have told him. I lied to him about my age on our third date, but he found the truth out and didn't even care that I was thirteen years older. "It makes you even more interesting to me," is what he said.

I think of my lies of omission. I never told Steven about the bottle of red wine I always keep in my clothes closet. When I finish one, I replace it. I never told him I'm still in touch with my old lover, George, or about my secret bank account, and then, before I can push it down, a great sadness washes over me as I think about the biggest lie I told him.

When Steven asked me why I did not have children I told him it never seemed like the right time. The story of the real reason why begins with a doctor in Astoria, Doctor Kaplan. I was a college freshman. It was the year before Roe vs. Wade was passed. For a charge of five dollars a visit, Dr. Kaplan scraped around inside my uterus with an instrument that looked like an oversize crochet hook. The procedure was supposed to work within three visits. Every time it did not work, I went back to see him again. The tenth time he also gave me an injection of something. I spent that night on all fours on my bed, my body wracked by terrible cramps. Just before dawn I expelled a bloody mass from between my legs. My boyfriend at the time, a junkie named Mark, took it into the bathroom and flushed it down the toilet. Years later, when I tried to get pregnant, I found out I could not, too much damage had been done. As the yogis and the rabbis and the stoned-out old hipsters all say, what goes around comes around.

I look at the clock again and am surprised to see I have been in Wheel pose for nine more minutes, instead of five. I slowly get out of it, stretch, get up. I still feel sad but also feel relaxed, lighter. I put water up for tea, then I go looking out the window. I see a group of well-dressed people, the men in suits, the women in fancy dresses and heels, out on the pier by the river. They are all carrying paper bags. I know they are Jews carrying their sins, symbolized by the bread in their bags. One by one they go to the guard rail and empty the bread into the water. I wish them Mazel Tov. Outside in the hall I hear Steven and Jack talking and laughing. Steven has a wonderful, booming laugh. Hearing it, I want to stay with him and see how far we can go. I decide to tell him about George, the wine in the closet, the secret bank account, the doctor in Astoria. I do not want any lies between us. In the New Year, I will have more than enough to deal with. I need to overcome my greed and selfishness. I need to get better at giving and accepting love and still keep my balance on this earth which whirls beneath my uncertain feet like a spinning wheel.

Delilah

Steven untied my wrists, which he had tied together behind my back with the belt from his bathrobe, then he untied my ankles, which he had bound together with my tights. He turned his attention to my nipples. They were sore where he had chewed and bit them. He kissed them tenderly, first one then the other, then his lips traveled up my neck, up my throat to my mouth.

"Open your eyes, open your eyes, look at me," he said before he put his lips on mine. I opened my eyes as we kissed and looked into his. In them I saw sapphires shining in blue skies. I don't know what he saw in mine, maybe oriental rugs, teapots, apples. When the kiss ended, he said, "I'll go out and get us food, Angel." I nodded yes. He left, but not before bringing me some water and kissing me again.

When we cause each other pain, when we play these rough sex games, the result seems at the end to be greater tenderness. We feel more relaxed with each other.

I want to call my mother on the phone and say, "See, Ma, kinky sex is saving my marriage," but I know she would not understand. She would be worried and think I am drinking. Steven and I are using our bodies to explore a brave new world, but maybe that, like so many promises of salvation, will lead us to a nightmare place devoid of sentiment and conscience. Who knows?

All I know is that the next time I want him to take the black leather belt he uses to hold up his jeans and run it back and forth slowly between my legs until it is wet and smells of my juices, then I want him to beat me with the belt until my ass turns red, then I want him to strap it across my lips like a gag, buckle it around my head and take me from behind.

I stretch and look down at my body. It is rosy and seems to glow. I am so relaxed I can barely raise my head. My nerve endings have gone to Morocco, maybe they are not coming back. I wonder if this how Sampson felt when he tried to rise from the bed of love, discovered himself shorn, and could not. The way that Delilah betrayed Sampson was that after she found out that his strength resided in his hair, she wooed him to sleep in their bed. While he slumbered there, she brought in a man to shave off Sampson's hair. When his skull was bare, she called in the Philistines. Sampson no longer had the strength to defend himself. They put out his eyes, bound him in chains, took him to Gaza and made him a slave. For her part in this treachery, they gave her a hundred pieces of silver.

The story of Sampson and Delilah reminds me that the more I give myself over to love, the more I can loose. Because of love I have fallen off the wall many times, curled back inside myself like a snail, wrecked my car, given myself terrible haircuts with rusty razor blades and now here I am in love again, this time with Steven, but this time I am trying something different, something radical, pretending to be the puppet, the slave, the doormat, the tool or the brute, because I can see how, if you do not act out the viciousness inside you, it can kill you. When we play our S&M games we always establish a safe word like "Danger" or "Red." He always stops when I say the word and so do I when I am the one in power.

You have to be very careful about whom you choose to play with, but even then you are always in danger because Delilah's ghost is everywhere. She multiplies, divides. Her succubae are very beautiful, skilled in the art of disguise. They live in the heart of every Bluebeard. They can thin themselves into a whisper, creep behind your eyes, get you to believe your lover is unfaithful, get you to believe he lies.

I know that Steven loves me, wants to hang in together and go the distance. Yet, I am so jealous. I mock him, I test him. Delilah the demon has snuck inside my head again. She says he is a Casanova, a creep who is using me although he brings me roses, coffee in bed, pumpernickel-raisin bread from Dean and De Luca.

A week ago at Jayne's crowded birthday party, I was having a conversation with a man who said he was an exterminator and who was wearing three silver rings through the center of his nose. He was telling me I could never subdue my suicidal urges by writing poetry. I excused myself and went to the food table for salsa and chips. As I was loading up a plate, I glanced around the room and saw Steven seated on a couch in the far corner of the room with a woman who had breasts the size of watermelons. I am a 32A. They were looking into each other's eyes and he had his hand on her knee. So much blood rushed into my head, all I could see was red. When my eyes cleared, I reached out, clutched the bowl of salsa around the edge. Maybe I would have hurled it at them but I was saved by three young men who came right up to me just then to tell me how much they liked my columns in Downtown and inadvertently pinned me against the table. While they were talking at me, Steven came over and joined us. I was so furious that I could not look into his cheating face and I did not speak to him all the way home in the car.

"What's up, Angel? What's the matter?" he asked but I did not answer him until we got home. Only then did I tell him what I saw. We had a huge fight. He said he wanted only me, that I was being crazy, jealous. He accidently touched her knee while making a point in conversation. I said I never noticed him accidently touching the knee of a man while making a point in conversation. He said I was behaving a like a child, so what if he touched her knee, he didn't kiss her or even take her hand. He was always trying to find new ways to show how much he cares for me. Don't I ever notice?

"You don't love me," I yelled, and ran into the bathroom and locked the door behind me because I didn't want to admit that I might be wrong. I waited in the bathroom until I heard him go out and only then did I open the door, come out to wander around the apartment looking for my better self. I looked in the closet, pulled open all the drawers, but I could not find her. I have always been jealous out of all proportion, maybe because my father used to step out on my mother or maybe because I don't believe I am beautiful. I wonder if Delilah is so powerful that she has bewitched me completely and I will never be free of jealously. I remember a program I heard on public radio. A sex positive feminist was saying how acting out your fantasies can help you to lead a healthy life. Repressing them can turn you into a Jeffrey Dahmer. I couldn't help thinking that if anyone was ever acting out his fantasies, it was Jeffrey Dahmer. I don't know what a healthy life is or even if there is such a thing. I do know that I want to escape the curse of Delilah. I want to transcend my jealousy and craziness and take it higher.

Steven came back in after three a.m. He did not find me sleeping. He found me sitting in his big rocking chair wearing one of his white muscle tee shirts, my thigh-high black fishnet stockings and my red stiletto heels. His mouth opened in surprise when he saw me but before he could say anything, I stood up, turned my back to him and displayed my ample rear.

"I know I've been a bad girl," I said, "and I deserve a spanking. Punish me for being a bad girl. Please spank me, spank me now."

"I will," he said. "Oh yes." He sat down on the chair, pulled me face down over his knees. He put one hand under the tee shirt and grabbed me securely by the breast. He used the other hand to spank hard with his big flat palm until I begged for mercy.

"I'll show you mercy," he said. He stood up, carried me to the bed where he threw me down on my side and took me from the back. He kept pounding into me so hard it was amazing the bed didn't collapse. I must have come at least five times before he exploded into me.

Now he is out getting us food and I am lying here with that funky smell of sex rising between my legs and hoping that at least temporarily we have found a way to keep Delilah and her legions of succubae at bay.

The Leopard Coat

I go over to Ursula's wearing the vintage real leopard fur coat I found at the bottom of the underwear bin at the Goodwill Store for fifteen dollars. It was ripped up both sides to where the sleeves connected to the arms, but I mended it. It is cut so that it flares out at the back and it has a big collar that I can turn up high as my ears. When I put it on, I feel so elegant and feline, like Greta Garbo in *Mata Hari* or Marlene Dietrich in *A Foreign Affair*. Maybe, when I wear the coat in the street, animal activists will pelt me with rotten eggs but I don't care.

Ursula pronounces the coat divine. I tell her she can borrow it anytime, maybe she will have a date with Johnny Depp. Ursula puts up water for tea then gets out her little soapstone pipe out of her jeans pocket and packs it with grass from the white porcelain sugar bowl she keeps on the table. She lights up, tokes and passes the pipe to me.

While she is preparing the tea, Ursula tells me that Patti is having an affair with John whom Ursula dated for three months last year right after he separated from his wife Laura. Ursula goes on to say that Patti and John came over to visit her and suggested a threesome. She politely declined because Patti is about as attractive to her as Elsie the cow, and she adds that she doesn't think Patti even cares for John and is only fucking him because Patti's live-in boyfriend Cliff is having an affair with Franny, the woman who works in the art supply store. At least Laura is not pining for John, she is having a passionate affair with a woman she met in her Tai-Chi class. I tell Ursula that this reminds me of the French farce, *La Ronde,* about a sexual musical chairs played among a group of friends. If you really love someone, I say, how can you enjoy sleeping with someone else? I say when you play with your passions, you play with fire.

Ursula responds by telling me that sex and love are two different things and vive la difference. She says sex just for the fun of it without emotional entanglement can be the as-good-as-it-gets. I disagree. I tell her it is the emotional connection that enriches sex or dooms it and even when the sex is casual or bad there is some kind of emotional connection or component. That can't be denied. That kind of behavior is like a false bravado, like trying to pretend you are cool when actually you are frightened. We drink our tea in silence, and then she says she is surprised at me. Since when have I gotten so judgmental of other people? Have I picked it up from Steven? She and Steven don't get along. "It's no crime to need sex, that good old sexual healing." She adds, "Sometimes we do what we need to in order to get through."

"Through what?" I ask, "Inability to make a commitment?" Ursula shakes her head, but says nothing, instead she lights the pipe again, passes it to me. I have not told her about the problems Steven and I are having or about how we have been trying to patch things up with sexual role-playing.

As I walk down Hudson Avenue on the way home from Ursula's, I think about what a mess I am in. I have long believed that no one can belong to anyone else, but since my marriage to Steven, I do feel that he belongs to me and that I belong to him. It's not a feeling I like. I used to believe marriage, at its best, was a series of compromises, yet I married Steven. I hate the expression "hooked up," but that's what happened. I got hooked up with him. I let it happen, and now it's not working. Our sex games have offered only a brief respite. Our marriage is in danger, I don't feel safe. I wrap my temptress coat around me as if it can keep me safe from my confusion.

A good-looking guy in a black jeep opens the window, leans his head out and whistles at me. "Want to go for a ride?" he yells out. I try not to look at him. I look straight ahead as if I hadn't heard or as if I am from Albania and don't understand English. He rolls up the window and speeds by. I find myself wondering what would have happened if I'd said, "Sure."

Would we go to some Ramada Inn over the George Washington Bridge in New Jersey or would we drive to the parking lot at Riis Park beach and do it in the back of the jeep. Then I think of Steven and how hooked up, for better or for worse, we are. I cannot really imagine anyone else inside me. If I fucked someone else, I'd feel wretched.

I already know. I know because of Tim and Gordon and me. I was twenty-seven and Tim was nineteen. I picked him up in a grocery store where he was buying a bottle of catsup. My friends were shocked when I took him to live with me. They thought he was too young, that it was an Oedipus situation, but if anything, he mothered me. He was the one who shopped and cleaned, made me breakfast in the morning. He was a sweet and tender lover, but he could also keep going like pile driver. I felt completely relaxed and comfortable in bed.

Gordon worked in the health food store with me. He was older, cool and witty, played the harmonica, said I had a Mona Lisa smile. One time I went with him to his tiny studio apartment on East 9th Street. He made me fried spaghetti and then we had sex on the floor. As soon as he put it in me, I knew it was a mistake. I kept seeing Tim's face. I couldn't come. As soon as Gordon pulled out, I leaped up, put my clothes on and dashed out of there like a bat out of hell. I could not/would not tell Tim. Why hurt him? For weeks after that I felt wicked, doomed, sly like I was the devil's creature.

I don't want to go to bed with anyone else but Steven, I know if I did it with anyone else I would only think of Steven. Maybe all this is happening to us because I actually am a hypocritical devil's creature, but in another way. I sold my soul for a marriage when I don't believe in marriage, maybe I was pretending. I did it in order to feel normal, as if I didn't know that I can never be normal, my brains are too big for my head. I wonder what would have happened if I hadn't married Steven but we had continued to just live together, not that it maters now.

I open the door to find Steven beating our new kitten, Beast, with my hairbrush.

"Stop it," I yell. "Why are you doing that again?"

"He was eating your ficus plant," Steven answers.

"I don't care," I shriek and I dash over, grab Beast up into my arms and rock the tiny mewing creature against my chest. Yesterday I came in and found Steven beating Beast because Beast was sleeping on the bed. Steven has the notion that cats are unclean and spread disease, even though I have pointed out to him several times that Beast is always washing himself. The day before that, he beat Beast because Beast was drinking out of the toilet bowl.

"I don't want my hairbrush ever used for such a purpose ever again," I yell at Steven. "These beatings must stop. I will get some of that Cat-Away Spray and spray it around the plant, and then Beast won't want to go near it."

"Those sprays never work," he yells back. "Spare the rod and spoil the cat."

This gets me even more furious. "I can't continue to live with a cat beater," I answer. "What happened to you when you were a kid to make you so cruel to a defenseless animal?"

"I had a great childhood," he says.

"I don't believe you. No one has a wonderful childhood," I say. "Who beat you up, your big brothers, your mother or your father?"

"I'm your husband, you should respect me. Who taught you to be such a bitch?"

We have one of our bang-up fights, the first one since we have been playing our bed games. It ends with him going out and slamming the door behind him so hard the cups on the kitchen table rattle. I am alone, bouncing off the walls. Maybe I should beat him with my hairbrush and see how he likes it, but considering some of those bed games of ours, he might like it very much.

Maybe I should really shake things up between us and have an affair. I imagine myself doing my hair up in an elegant French twist, putting on my leopard coat and going to the Plaza Bar. I could pick up a powerful international businessman or an international spy, sort of a James Bond type. Then I suddenly realize how quickly I have changed my spots. On my way home from Ursula's house, right after talking like a prig with her about commitment, I fantasize about jumping in a jeep with a strange guy just because he whistles at me and now I'm doing that again, imagining a pick-up at the Plaza. No matter how many leopard coats I own, I wonder if I can ever be constant, ever be committed, even with my wedding ring on my finger.

Danger!

I rent a movie for my VCR in which Robert De Niro is the master criminal bad guy and Al Pacino the relentless detective good guy. Pacino gets De Niro in the end because De Niro goes back at the very last minute to get a snitch who ratted on him; one more deep breath and De Niro would have been home free but he just couldn't let it go.

Why do people hold on so tightly to anger and hate? I do it too, and why? I don't know. I get another wine cooler from the refrigerator and return to watch De Niro bleeding to death, his white shirt turning red. Like Pacino and De Niro, men cannot seem to resist shaking their sticks at each other, fighting about who has the biggest. Some feminists say that if women ruled the world, we would have peace, but judging by me it would not go that way.

No matter how many long, healthy walks I take, no matter how much I do yoga or meditate, I so easily become jealous, angry, full of rage. When I am hit, I still want to hit back like De Niro in the movie.

The fights Steven and I are having are getting more abusive and deranged. Our wild sex games no longer bring us any peace and in fact have abruptly ceased because I bit Steven so hard on his scrotum I broke the skin and drew blood. He says he told me "Danger! Danger, stop, stop, danger!" I didn't hear him, but how could I have not? Did I block the safe word out? He believes I did and says that this shows that deep down I wanted to castrate him. He called me an old witch and I called him a moron and a loser. Maybe it's all over between us, but we cannot seem to simply let it go, the word "simple" does not seem to have any place in the loony lexicon of our love. We didn't speak for two days after that.

I was talking about our problems with my brother and he suggested we go out for a special dinner, leave our neighborhood, pick a restaurant we had never been to before. My brother said this ploy had worked well for him and his wife more than once after a terrible argument. I suggested a night out away from our familiar surroundings and Steven agreed.

So last week, late Tuesday night, we were driving back from Sheepshead Bay, from Randazzo's Clam Bar. We had shared an excellent meal of Lobster Fra Diablo and steamed clams as well as a good bottle of Pinot Grigio. I had my hand on Steven's knee as he drove along. A nice idea came into my head. "Let's go away together weekend after next" I suggested, "It's our six-month wedding anniversary. I'll take off from the flea market. Maybe we could drive up to Woodstock and spend the night?"

Steven didn't answer for a minute. Then he said, "That weekend won't be good. I already told Gary I'd go with him and a couple of the guys from Milano's to the Catskills on a fishing trip. It's Gary's birthday."

"How come you didn't mention it to me?" I wanted to know. "Cancel it so we can go away."

"I already him told him yes," Steven said, "Why don't we go away the weekend after that?" Jealously, the green-eyed monster was already creeping around inside my head.

"It's our anniversary weekend," I said."That is more important."

"What's the big difference when we go, as long as we're together," he answered.

I couldn't admit that maybe he was right. Instead, I said, "So Gary and the guys are more important to you than I am?"

"There you go," he answered, "trying to control me again, selfish witch." From there it wasn't long until I told him to "Go fuck yourself and fuck your mother too." He jammed on the brakes and we skidded to a stop half-way through a red light. This was my cue to open the door and run out into the starless Brooklyn night. A second later the light changed and he drove away.

I saw a street sign that said Albemarle Road and realized that I was not in the best of neighborhoods. I was wearing a skimpy white t-shirt and a short black lace skirt that I put on because Steven likes it. My legs were bare and I was wearing white platform wedges. I knew Flatbush Avenue was around here somewhere, maybe I could catch a cab or take a bus. I lurched, weeping, down Albemarle Road to find Flatbush Avenue only a block away.

All of the stores were closed, protected by iron gates. I found the bus stop and I waited. A car full of men rode by, someone yelled out

"Pusss-y." A beer can thrown from the car lands at my feet. I pray for a taxi or a police car to approach. No luck. I try to make myself invisible by repeating the first line of the Lord's Prayer, which is all I can remember. "The lord is my shepherd and I shall not want" I say aloud over and over. I do not know if I still believe in the Lord, but I still believe in shepherds and maybe that is enough, because no one comes along to molest me as I stand on that desolate corner waiting for a bus that does not come for at least a half hour.

It's four A.M. when I get home and I go into my place and lock the door. Steven has his own space across the hall and we have each other's keys. He rents a studio a few blocks away where he works on his big sculptures. We patterned our marriage after the relationship of Sartre and Simone De Beauvoir, but I have since learned that I am not capable of the detachment an existential marriage takes. I fall out, exhausted, and then wake to find Steven standing over me, looking furious.

"Why did you run away like that?" he yells. "You put yourself in danger. Something bad could have happened to you running around late at night in a strange neighborhood." I'm groggy from sleep but find that I can yell too. "You were the one who put me in danger. Why did you just drive away and leave me?" I snap back.

"After I drove off, I knew it was wrong. I shouldn't have done that," he said. "I turned back and was driving around looking for you for a long time."

"You should have been able to find me," was my reply. "I was standing right on Flatbush Avenue waiting for a bus. Maybe you weren't looking hard enough?" I felt myself getting angry again. I was about to say, "Can't you do anything right?" but for once I caught myself. "Forget it," I said, "our wires were crossed. Let's just go to sleep. Tomorrow is another day."

Terminal Velocity

I do not want to write about my mother's increasing senility, her frightening decline. I do not want to write about my recent separation from my husband or the terrible fight that preceded it. I want to write about the end of the world and flaming Armageddon, about whole cities exploding, to explain why I am in this pain, why I find myself treading water in a river of fire.

I close my eyes and try to focus on my topic, try to visualize huge tidal waves engulfing Manhattan, but all I can see is my mother's anxious, lined face. We are in her kitchen four days ago during my solitary visit to Maryland. I am making my morning coffee and she is following me around the kitchen. Together we chant the bagel litany:

"Do you want a bagel?"

"No, Ma."

"Do you want a bagel?"

"No, Ma."

"Do you want a bagel?"

"No, Ma."

When she grows tired of that my mother switches to the Steven litany:

"How's Steven and you doing?"

"Fine, Ma."

"How's Steven and you doing?"

"Fine, Ma."

"How's Steven and you doing?"

"Fine, Ma."

She ask me the question about Steven and again and again and I keep on lying and saying "fine" until she stops and finds another question because Steven and I have been strip-mined and are not doing fine at all.

First there was that terrible fight we had when we were driving through a strange neighborhood late at night. Then last week we had such a row that we broke up. No, we are not doing fine at all.

After breakfast my mother falls asleep on the couch, snoring, her mouth open, her housecoat rolled up to show that, despite her illness, her lack of activity, she still has good legs. My father taps me on the shoulder and we go into their bedroom, sit down on their bed, which smells of Vicks Vaporub and sweat.

My mother was once an obsessive housecleaner, now my father says she no longer seems to care. She gets confused when she tries to change the sheets on the bed. He is very worried and so am I. Then the moment comes that I have been dreading and my father asks about Steven and me. I have to tell him the truth.

I take a deep breath and say that we have separated. Steven is living in his studio a few blocks away.

"Oh, no" my father says. He is all for Steven and looks at him as a shining knight who came along and saved me from an old age spent eating T.V. dinners. "What happened?" my father wants to know, "You two seemed so happy." I tell him that we fell into a terrible pattern of blame and recrimination but I don't tell him the details. I don't tell him how we couldn't stop hurting each other, how our fights grew worse and worse. We were both to blame. I am so sensitive I seem to have elephantiasis of the ego and Steven's way to solve a problem seems to be to smoke more pot. He was always complaining that we never spent weekends together. I work in the flea market on Saturdays and Sundays when he is off from his job. In an effort to save our marriage, I applied for an adjunct teaching job at a local university, but they never got back to me.

After the fight, when I jumped out of the car, we didn't even speak for a few days. I knew he was as shaken up as I was and I wanted to make up. I tried to get Steven to go to the beach with me. He kept saying that he didn't want to leave the air conditioning. One night he lies down in bed to watch TV with me. In the middle of Homicide, he tells me that his dick is hard. I say, "Can't you think of a more interesting approach?"

The next day, to make amends for cold cocking him, I buy him a dozen red roses and put them in a vase in front of the door to his room across the hall. When he comes in from his studio later, he comes over to my place, knocks on the door and when I open it he says, "Thanks for the flowers but you should save your money."I slammed the door in his face. Then, a few days a few days later, we had the biggest fight, the splitsville fight.

My father asks, "Can't you salvage it?" but I tell him that I don't know how. Once I start to rag on Steven, I am powerless to stop. I tell my father that my headshrinker is away in London so there is no help from that quarter. All my friends had advised me to separate because when they were around us they could see how vicious our interactions had become.

I inform my father that Steven and I had reached terminal velocity, which is one of the few terms I know from physics. It means that we have come to a place where we could not fall any faster or harder through space; then we hit the ground, we explode.

My father and I agree not to tell my mother at this time because it might give her a stroke. He says, "Don't worry honey, if you need money, just ask. Do what's best for you," but I can tell by the grave look on his face that I have doubled his worries and I feel very sad.

The next day, when I am visiting my brother, Julia, now seven, says, "Where is Steven? Why didn't you bring him? I want my Uncle Steven," while Matthew, now three, runs around the room playing a little ukulele Steven gave him.

Back in New York my apartment is very quiet, quiet as a tomb. I lie in bed drinking scotch, trying to get through the night. Wherever I look; on the ceiling, on the floor, I see Steven's face. I get up and, in an effort to cheer myself, put on my favorite Bob Marley tape, but the lyrics only mock me, "I want to love and treat you right, I want to be with you every night." I keep blaming myself; I'm good at talking about love but not good at making it. I know that blaming myself will only make it worse, but I can't stop. "Everything's going to be all right," Bob Marley sings out into my lonely room, but I do not believe him.

I can't stop thinking about that final fight and how casually, how insidiously it started. Steven came home from work and I poured him his usual evening scotch and a short one for myself. We talked about the trip to Maryland we were planning and the gifts we would bring. He wanted to get two stuffed pandas that he'd seen in a shop window for the kids. I said that sounded great. Then he told me that his ex-wife just called him from Toronto. She was coming down to New York tomorrow for a few days for a convention. She wanted to see him, had something she wanted to tell him. Her father just died, and she was feeling very low.

"Okay," I say, "let's invite her to dinner and after dinner I'll leave, take a drive or go visit Ursula," but he says no. At first I am perplexed, but then I can see how the idea of spending an evening with wife number one and wife number two at the same time could be overwhelming. I suggest we all meet in a bar for a cocktail and after one drink I split. I say that seems to be a highly evolved, a very Aquarian, very Zen way to deal with the situation of meeting the "ex" of a spouse, but he says no again. I feel myself getting angry. I want to know why. He does not reply and over the next couple of days I find I cannot let it go.

I even hear myself asking him if he is ashamed of me and he tells me it makes him sick to hear me talking so. I wonder what is going on. Does he still have feelings for her? During a fight last month he told me he was much happier when he was married to her. My paranoia, if it is that, is not decreased by the fact that when I was a teenager my father began a long affair with a woman he used to date before he met my mother.

I yell at Steven, tell him he is disrespecting me. I say we are going to break up over this, but all I get in reply is a stony silence. After a while I realize I am getting crazy. It is not worth it. I tell him I feel excluded but will respect his feelings even though I cannot figure out what they are. He says he has made a dinner date with her for Saturday evening and I say okay.

Saturday, he comes in to my place about five o' clock. He is wearing the navy blue silk dress shirt that I got for him and his tuxedo pants. He looks divine. He tells me he will be meeting her at six and he won't be home late.

I mope about the house, clean out my make-up drawer, strip, put Crimson Sunset lipstick on my nipples. I will surprise him when he gets home, put on my black high heels and greet him at the door naked and with a big kiss. Why not make a fresh approach? As John Lennon said, love is all you need. When he is not back at eleven o'clock, I get out of bed, where I have been lying naked and waiting, dress and go out to get a fresh bottle of scotch before the liquor store closes at midnight.

I come home, check the answering machine, but he has not called. I open the new bottle and by 1:30 a.m. it is half gone, I am more than a little frantic and I cannot keep from crossing the hall and using my key to go into the two rooms across the hall where he keeps his clothes and has fashioned a little den with for himself with desk and couch. Everything looks the same, his clothes piled neatly on the shelves he made above the fake fireplace. Here and there, pinned to the walls, are dried roses I have given him. I go sit on the couch and there on the table, next to the phone, I see his wedding ring.

During our last rash of quarrels he had taken it off, but recently he had started to wear it again. Now it was shining up at me, glowing golden but empty next to a book of matches from Veselkas. The familiar green demon of jealously has invaded my head. He punches my eyes, kicks me in the teeth. I get up and flail around the room, tear down the roses tacked to the wall, pick up the ficcus plant I gave him, and throw it across the room. I break a vase that sits on his table, kick a mirror he was refinishing for me into smithereens. When Steven comes in at four a.m., I am weeping on the floor, surrounded by mirror shards, dried rose petals, cracked glass.

He calls me a lunatic, a nut case. I yell, "Why didn't you call me, why didn't you wear your wedding ring?" He says he didn't feel like it. I call him a bastard but then we both realize there is no sense in yelling anymore, there is nothing left to say. I stumble back across the hall into to my place and crash out on the floor. When I wake up in the bright sunlit room there are a few moments when I don't even know where I am, but then I remember the events of the night before and my stomach starts to heave and churn, it is so full of bile. I go into the bathroom and puke it all up.

I do not know how this could have happened to us, but I will have plenty of time to figure it out, because when I come out of the bathroom I find a note shoved under my door. It says "Will move to my studio while you go see your family."There is also a little white envelope, which holds a wedding ring. This is terminal velocity for sure.

Cheating Heart

I have not seen or heard from Steven since my return from Maryland. Meanwhile, it is business as usual. No matter how often I clean the cat litter, the box still stinks. My? our? the? cat Beast knocks over the VCR and I do not have the money to fix it. At night I try to sleep while Beast, curled on top of the covers, snores and thrashes his paws. Maybe, somewhere in his dreams, he will catch the bluebird of no regrets and bring it to me. I try to masturbate myself to sleep but all my fingers turn into thumbs. I hurt myself and do not come and I remember how Celine said that when masturbation provides neither comfort nor entertainment, you are really in despair.

Ursula calls. She invites me to go with her to Balzano's, in Red Hook. "It's Friday night," she says. "There will be dancing."

I am sick of my solitary misery, sick of waiting for the phone to ring. Every time it does ring my belly does flip-flops and then, when it is not Steven, I feel like throwing up. I need to get far away from that phone. I say yes to Ursula, fine, and then I lie down in bed and put moist chamomile tea bags over my eyes to reduce the redness and swelling. When I feel better, I get up, eat half a jar of peanut butter and dress for my evening out. I put on my black satin toreador pants and white lace top. I want to look hot and not like a woman who has been crying herself to sleep for two weeks.

Balzano's is long and narrow. The bar runs all the way up one wall. Booths are on the other side; dancing takes place in the aisle. The music is provided by Big Cliff. His name is a joke, because he is only five foot two. He plays guitar and sings a mixture of country and rock. As Ursula and I enter he is belting out "Your cheating heart will tell on you."

Sunny, the bartender, comes over as soon as we sit down. "Hi, good-looking," he says,

"I haven't seen you for a while." Jackie Sousa, who was sitting with Fred and Mary Jane in a booth, comes over. "Where's Steven?" she asks. I say that we had a big fight and that he is staying in his studio, although I actually don't know where he is. "You must be kidding," she says, "you guys were so much in love."I tell her, "Thanks a lot."

A few gin and tonics later I am dancing with a man named Richard. He is tall, older, with silver hair. He says he remembers dancing with me here a few years ago. He tells me he came back to the bar looking for me but I was gone. I don't remember him. I wonder if this is just his line, but I like dancing with him, he's good with his long legs like Fred Astaire. We sit together at the bar. I let him buy me a drink. He says he is glad he has found me.

I tell him that I am married now but it is not going well. I do not tell him that my husband and I are separated. Richard glances at my left hand and sees my wedding ring. I am still wearing it because I can't bear to take it off. I know that is a hurdle that I must cross soon, particularly since Steven has already given his ring back to me.

Richard takes a dollar bill from the wallet in his pocket and writes his phone number across George Washington. He hands it to me. "Keep this in case you want some company," he says. "I would love to take you out for dinner, we could drive out to the Rockaways, walk along the beach, maybe we could have dinner out there. Even if you just want to talk, call anytime at all. I'm available, I don't want to loose touch with you."

As we drive home, Ursula says, "Richard is a dream." I tell her I must see how things go with Steven. She asks me why. This is a good question, since I left three messages on his answering machine in the last week saying "let's talk" and he hasn't called back. She goes on, "What are you waiting for?" she asks. "Do you think he'll stop smoking pot? You need to move on."

I know she's right but I tell her that it's too soon. I'm not ready to date someone else yet. I want to talk with Steven. I have to talk with him. She starts to sing, "if you can't be with the one you love, love the one you're with." She can't carry a tune. In order to get her to stop, I cut in with, "Your cheating heart will tell on you." I can't carry a tune either.

When I get home, I take off my clothes and fall into bed. I still feel married to Steven, I wonder whether, if I went to bed with Richard, I would feel as though I was cheating. The refrain, cheating heart, keeps running through my brain. The song has an old association for me. It was the name of Bobby Black's boat. He was a Chesapeake Bay waterman I met on a visit to my brother ten years ago.

We met in a bar called The Ugly Buzzard while he was delivering oysters. He shucked a dozen oysters for me and told me that watching me down those oysters was the prettiest sight he had ever seen.

Later that night, Bobby Black and I headed off to the guest bedroom in my brother's house. He said that he lived on his boat and didn't have a telephone so he would have to call me. When I got back to New York, he called sometimes twice a day.

Soon he came up for a visit. We did it on my kitchen floor, on the couch, in my bed and in the shower, causing a flood that made my downstairs neighbors come up and pound on the door. We were eating pepperoni pizza and planning a trip to Puerto Rico when the phone rang. It was my brother, very upset. He told me that an extremely pregnant woman had just come into his antique shop. She was weeping. She begged him to tell me I was ruining her marriage. She showed him a picture of her and Bobby and their three-year-old son, Bobby Jr., smiling on the deck of The Cheating Heart.

I told Bobby what my brother had told me. Bobby said that it was true but that he was in love with me and was going to leave her and their son. I said, "Sure, like shit doesn't attract flies and the moon is blue." I threw him out and told him never to call me again.

Pond Scum

I go to the sauna with my old friend Nancy. She is ashamed because her boyfriend, Ando, ran off with her sister last week. She doesn't want anyone to know how she has been cuckolded.

We are both in a crazed state. I cannot stop thinking about Steven, who is not communicating with me. Nancy and I agree that we are feeling castrated, devastated and constipated all at once. She is crying, blaming herself because she thinks she didn't pay enough attention to Ando. I tell that her no matter how lopsided it may look, when a couple splits the responsibility is always fifty-fifty. I do not tell her how guilty I feel because of the times I used to deny Steven sex in a futile effort to control him. Instead, I tell her people are too screwed up to have "healthy" relationships these days.

While I am talking I notice that the sauna is not clean and that a faint green scum covering one quarter of the wooden floor appears to be creeping towards me. It looks like the pond scum that my friend Michael Carter recently told me is covering eighty-eight percent of America's fresh water ponds. I tell Nancy that the whole world is fucked, we might as well blame the pond scum. Maybe it is clouding everyone's eyes so that issues cannot be seen clearly, maybe it is covering our tongues, making it impossible to communicate, clogging up our personal and political lives.

I tell Nancy that last night I watched the presidential debates and saw a wooden man with a bronze star where his heart should have been trading mealy mouth digs with a puff pastry JFK wannabe. It would have been more interesting to watch electric eels mate. Nancy did not watch the debate. She spent the evening crying and trying to shit. I asked her, "What do you think is dirtier, relationships or politics?" We both laughed, ha-ha-ha, even though the question was not funny.

She asked me how Michael Carter was because she knew that he had been beaten and arrested by the NYPD for verbally protesting the curfew in Tompkins Square Park. I told her he was fighting back, had taken the case to the courts, although our courts are probably as awash in pond scum as the rest of America. How could our courts have let the Mayor impose the new, stricter parking regulations that have resulted in me getting over 500 dollars worth of parking citations in the last two months?

If I were truly a terrorist, I would gain access to the mayor's office by saying I had smoked crack with Al Sharpton and was ready to go public. Once inside I would take the mayor by surprise, I would subdue him by spraying him with Chanel #5, I would then bend him over his desk, pull his pants down and ram my 500 dollars worth of parking tickets up his big fat wazoo. Instead, I stay in the sauna and try to sweat this insidious pond scum out of my head, but no can do.

I leave Nancy in the sauna, shower, exit the Russian and Turkish Baths with my shit still in a knot and my brains still in a witches brew.

On the sidewalk outside is a woman with a shopping cart filled with dishes, pots, pans, books, clothes. She can't be more than thirty, but she has only two teeth left in her mouth and those teeth are green and covered with a mossy substance that looks, and I am not surprised, like pond scum. There is something familiar about her; maybe in a former life we were both whores in Casablanca or maybe in a former life she was my Siamese twin. She has put some garments out to sell on the sidewalk. There is a not-all-that-shabby black, hooded sweatshirt with the word "Champion" emblazoned on it in bright turquoise letters. Maybe wearing it will give me the courage to finish my Saint Kevorkian poem. I kneel, but as I put my handout to touch it, my hand is suddenly shoved aside by a wooden club.

"Put that down Miss. She's moving on," a hoarse voice says. I look up to see a reed-slim young cop with a thin, pointy face like a rat.

"Pick it up, you scumbag," he says to the poor woman. I want to protest, say she is a human being, she deserves courtesy, but then I remember Michael Carter. I don't want to be beaten, arrested; I am frightened so I say nothing. The woman scrambles about picking up her stuff and throwing it in her cart. She hurries away.

"Get out of here, Miss," the policeman says to me. He turns and moves down the block. My fears root me to the spot, and I am sure, if I turn my head the slightest measure to the right, the pond scum will wash over me.

The End of the World

At poetry readings people come up to me and chirp too brightly, "How are you? You look so go-o-o-d," the good stretching out like pulled taffy, a sugary little bon mott to console me for my break-up with Steven. Perhaps they expect me to look like a witch out of Macbeth, all gaunt, hollow-eyed and gray, which is how I feel inside. I have discovered over the last month that if I put on enough Max Factor Under-Eye Magic Cover-Up and pile on the tangerine blush, my wretched, shredded libido doesn't show.

People don't know what to say; better luck next time sounds cruel. Everyone seems relieved I'm not vilifying him in public, calling him a bastard and weeping into my wine. However, when Ellen comes up to me at the Big Voices, Small Presses Book Fair to compliment me on my new high-heeled sneakers she "casually" mentions that she ran into Steven at Milano's where he was drinking with a gorgeous woman whom he introduced as Rita. Ellen then adds that she ran into them again the next morning having breakfast at Aggie's. I feel like tearing her tongue out. I run out the door and down Forty-Fourth Street crying like a banshee. I feel like it is the end of the world.

I tell my friends about this new development. They murmur soothing cliches like "this should give you some closure," while I mutter obscenities like "ratfink, weasel cock, asshole." My father has been urging me to make a bridge to Steven, to keep calling him. He suggests I should leave "let's talk" messages on Steven's answering machine.

When my father phones up to see how I am doing, I tell him about Steven and Rita. He says, "Oh, no, no, no. Do you need anything Duchess? Maybe you should get some new clothes, a haircut? Go out, have a good time. Maybe if Steven hears you are not pining for him, he will come around." I tell my father, "Thank you, but I don't need any new clothes." I don't tell him that since the news about Steven and Rita I haven't felt much like going out and socializing.

A week later I get a check from my father for 200 dollars. What a guy! I cash the check and go to the hair salon at Saks Fifth Avenue. They give me champagne to drink and the stylist, Jean-Paul, colors my hair platinum blonde and gives me a striking Jean Harlow haircut. On the way out I buy a Lady Luck red lipstick at the Chanel counter. I still have enough money left to buy a big bottle of Stoli vodka, 100 proof.

An invitation to an art opening arrives in the mail from a woman I met at a party named Amanda. Her show is called "Future Musings." I am delighted with this opportunity to show off my new lipstick and hairstyle. The gallery is in a townhouse on Madison Avenue, very ritzy with marble floors. I arrive wearing my black leggings, a red sweater and my motorcycle jacket. The other women are wearing cocktail dresses and velvet gowns. The men are wearing elegant suits.

The "Future Musings" are red explosions on black backgrounds with disembodied distorted white skulls popping out of them here and there. To my eyes they have no grace or beauty and are not ugly enough to be interesting. Maybe it is some kind of a put-on but no one is laughing and people are standing around in front of the paintings discussing them in hushed tones like they were Picassos.

I find the artist, introduce myself, remind her how we met at Mary's party. She limply presses my hand while looking over my shoulder. It's obvious she has no idea who I am. I wander around, trying to make eye contact with someone, anyone, but I have become invisible. I go to the back of the gallery where an immaculate white cloth has been spread over a mammoth desk to make a bar presided over by a clean-cut guy with a shaved head. He at least seems to see me because he smiles and fills a glass with red wine and slides it over to me. As I reach to pick it up, my hands fumble and I knock the glass down, spilling the red wine over the white cloth, which now resembles a bloody sheet.

The people who have been chatting, waiting for drinks, behind me, fall silent.

"I'm so sorry," I sputter out. Shaved head, no longer smiling, says, "That's all right," but it is not and I exit the gallery. Outside it has gotten colder and it is raining. I walk to the subway, feeling miserable once again like it is the end of the world. As I am waiting to cross the street a jeep drives by and splashes me. The receding license plate says "CRIMINAL."

The next morning Ursula calls and invites me to Balzano's that evening. I think about the nice man, Richard whom I had met there a while back. Shortly after I got the dread news about Steven and Rita I looked in my wallet for the dollar bill he gave me with his phone number on it only to discover that I had spent it. Maybe Richard will drop by Balzano's this evening, I tell Ursula yes.

The bar is crowded and smoky. There seem to be four men for every woman. Ursula whispers in my ear, "Have we died and gone to heaven or what?" Then, quicker than you can say "hot to trot," a short blond guy who looks like a kewpie doll comes up to me and says,

"Hello, pretty lady." He introduces himself as Billy and, after I tell him my name, we stand in the crowd while he tries to entertain me with stories of his job. He is a construction engineer, travels to exotic places like Egypt and Maracaibo. His breath is sweet, his fingernails are clean, his feet are big but something is missing. I don't feel bathed in moonlight, he doesn't turn me on.

He invites me out for lunch. I tell him no thanks. He starts to whine, "but why, why not?" I tell him I have to go to the ladies room. Once inside, perched on the throne, I do long, deep slow Yoga breathing to clear my mind. I remind myself nothing ventured, nothing gained. I head back into the fray.

I see an empty barstool, grab it, and try to look relaxed when I am not. I order double vodka, and down it quickly. I find myself thinking that since no one is noticing me maybe I should seize the moment, attract some attention. I could leap onto the bar and do a slow striptease while I recite the Gettysburg Address. However, I do not act on this. Someone cuts the jukebox and the band begins to play Hotel California.

The drummer is attractive with a long black ponytail and dancing eyes. I decide to be the bold one this time. After the set I approach him, tell him how much I like the way he keeps the beat. Soon we are talking about music, the sixties, the new psychedelic drugs, none of which I have tried. Then he asks me if I'm allergic to cats. I say no, surprised, ask him why. He says, "Because you're invited to my place tonight to try some ecstasy and fuck." I'm taken aback. Maybe I am indeed old-fashioned, but I believe in courtship, at least a preliminary cup of coffee or a shared doughnut. I ask him, "Do you always invite women to spend the night with you after you know them only five minutes?" He shrugs his shoulder, "Sure," he says, "why not?" and then he turns and moves away.

"Why not?" indeed, he has a point. After all, such a question is not the end of the world. I find Ursula talking with a guy wearing a fur

Davey Crockett hat who looks like he has been out in the woods too long. This is none of my business and I sit down at the bar and order another drink. In the mirror across from the bar I see my reflection. I see a good- looking woman with a great haircut and I smile at her. At least this evening has proved to me that I can still attract suitors and that being a woman who goes out alone is not the end of the world.

Dating Dylan Thomas

I have longed to move away from the hissing of the spent lie, and the old terrors continual cry growing more terrible as the day moves over the hill into the deep sea... — Dylan Thomas, "I Have Longed To Move Away"

I

I spend whole days reading ads in the newspapers for machinery that has no place in my *tabula rasa* life; anti-curl fax machines with auto paper-cutters and Motorola beepers that vibrate. I lay around in my stretched-out undies, the cheapest skullduggery of rayon acetate, my skimpy tits in a saggy old bra. My poetry is dull and full of lonely longing. My crush on Dylan Thomas can generate no real heat and I'm tired of hunting through gloomy bars for a sex machine with the soul of a poet.

Because Dylan Thomas says poetry comes out of life, I decide I'm going to accept the next date I'm offered, even though dating has not been my destiny. My destiny has been panhandling on Mission while Peter nodded out in our old Con Edison van. My destiny has been drinking acid punch at a party in the Provincetown pinewoods, falling for the man playing the congas, and living with him till he died by drowning. My destiny has been going to bed with Galahad and all his friends, learning to tell the difference in a pitch-dark room between the smell of a scrotum and the smell of a bottle of Jack Daniels oozing out with post coital sweat. My destiny has been a good Catholic boy who didn't know what he was getting into, an Arab street peddler who said I was made for his pleasure, a hillbilly from Tennessee who turned out to be a crack addict, a boy toy who liked to wear my bustier and make me bark like a dog. But dating never interested me. I might have dated Dylan Thomas, met him for cocktails, ridden through Central Park with him in a hansom cab, but I suspect dating was not his destiny either.

II

At Max Fish, Steve Modell reads about how, when he was fifteen, he got buggered by an old junkie queen. The guy behind the bar has big goofy, gooey chocolate eyes; can't take those eyes off me. He presents me with an encouraging bulge in his jeans; maybe it's padded. He asks for my number, breathing hard. I slip him my card. Find meat on bones that will soon have none is what Dylan Thomas says.

The next day Big Eyes calls, says his name is Cleese and could I please, please go out with him that night. His importunities make me feel like I do when I wear high heels; I can still strut and kick butt. I tell him I'm very busy, oh so busy. I don't tell him what I'm busy at is reading the ads in the newspapers. I know I'm playing a rotten, stalling game and the name of the game is fear of intimacy equals death in life. I force myself to agree to meet him for a date that very night at The Idiot's Delight. I prune my pubic hair, dust off my dimples. When I put on my make-up, I see I resemble Elizabeth Taylor. An eternal beauty, that's what I am.

Cleese is not at Idiot's Delight when I arrive. The room is crowded with idiots, morons, would-be virgins, poseurs and women wearing black dresses and black platform shoes. I grab the only available table in the back by the men's room door. When the waiter asks for my order, he calls me "Ma'am," a verbal kick in the crotch that always destroys me. Eternal beauties are properly called "Miss." or perhaps "Ms." I order a glass of house red and by the time Cleese arrives I have downed it. That may be why he appears bathed in a rosy glow, shining from head to toe in youthful testosterone.

I feel like a phony trying to be flirtatious with him when what I want to say is, "Let's just slip under the table and do it, we won't be noticed. In places like this no one looks below the crotch." Instead I ask him if staring at a woman is his usual way of making contact and is that why he has such big eyes. He leans towards me and takes one of my hands in both of his. "You have an aura that turns me on," he says. "I want to make love to you. I want to live with you." Suddenly in his goofy eyes I see an imaginary room, a funky old round oak table, a blue coffee pot, a couple of rocking chairs. He starts to tell me about his life. He's twenty-seven, left a wife and three-year-old son in Amsterdam. When I ask him how old the wife is, he says "Fifty." He tells me he came to New York with a clothing designer who got Parkinson's and had to go into a nursing home.

"Poor lady," I say, "to get sick so young."

"Well, she was sixty-one," he says. He begins to look shifty, smaller and smaller. Then he tells me he split from his last great love two months ago. She was an opera singer with a twenty-year-old son. He was shrinking quickly, diminishing before my eyes.

"How old was this one," I asked him, "Sixty-five?"

"Oh, no," he says. "She was sixty-two."

The imaginary room drops into a black hole in space. If an old woman is what he wants, let him go to a geriatric center. I am eternally young like Elizabeth Taylor, I am, I am. My whole life has been a war waged against categorical thinking, and now I am wasting time sitting across the table from a man who would love me more for my aging face than my graceful turn of mind, so much for dating.

Cleese was saying something about the spirituality of Native Americans. I cut in and tell him there is something about his aura that turns me off. I throw a fiver on the table for my wine. As I rise from my chair, I hear a loud sneeze. I look up and there is Dylan Thomas coming out the men's room door zipping up his fly. He catches my eye. It was him all right, the receding chin and puffy gullet, the heavy-lidded, beady eyes, the kinky hair. He had the pasty face and pear-shaped body of one who spends long hours sitting down indoors. His eyes are not the Celtic ice blue I have always imagined, but pale light green, green like gooseberries. He points with his head towards the door. As I make my way out of the crowded restaurant he is right behind me.

"Scuse me, scuse, scuse" he mutters as he jostles tables, tinkles crockery. I push out the door into the street. He grabs my arm and pulls me over to the streetlight; he isn't much taller than I am in my clumsy clogs. He bends towards me inspecting my face intently with those glistening, gooseberry eyes. He opens his mouth to speak and I shrink back expecting the fetid stink of death and decay, instead his breath smells of roses and pineapples.

"You're a wee bit long in the tooth," he says, "but you are a robin-breasted tree. Your glowing branches sparkle; you did right leaving that snit of a boy. Think of all the good men who have loved you." I think of drowned Dickie O. He could chart a course by the stars across the Provincetown dunes all the way to Africa. I think of Davidson who called me Pussy Heaven and held me in his long arms when we slept. I think about how hard we tried to make it together, but we couldn't stop fighting. We have been split up ten years now; every year since then he has sent me an orchid on my birthday.

"Take love where you find it, you galloping, glorious girl," Dylan Thomas says. He kisses me deep with his fruity rosy breath until a familiar sap spreads between my legs.

"Blessings on the wild child," he adds, then vanishes. The street is deserted except for a loony wino bodhisattva sitting cross-legged and grinning on a piece of cardboard in front of the futon store. My knees are shaking and my palms have begun to sweat. I need another drink. I will go to my favorite bar, the Right Bank in Williamsburg, which, despite all the rumors of imminent closing, had miraculously managed to stay open. I drive shakily over the bridge; all the while the car reeks of pineapples.

When the bartender, Mel, sees me come in, he pours my usual cup of cold sake.

Soon I am floating along on a sake sampan; little kernels of rice are in my shoes, leftovers from everyone else's weddings. I want to kick off my shoes and dance on the bar, singing "I am an eternal beauty, I am, I am, I am a robin-breasted tree."Someone touches my arm. It is Owen, someone I had talked to once a couple months ago. He has a good strong back and a mouth like a cherry, but he is oh, so young.

"How are you doing?" he asks.

"I am a robin-breasted tree," I tell him.

"I know it," he says. "Why don't you ever talk to me? I look at women all the time, but I never see anyone who excites me like you. I want to get to know you better."

"Are you making fun of me?" I ask, "Or are you some weirdo who goes for women old enough to be your mother? Do you know how old I am?"

"I have some idea," he says, "but I'm in no position to make fun of anybody. I don't care if you're twenty or thirty or sixty or eighty. I want to be with you. Take me home with you."

An hour later, in my messy kitchen, I pull my mouth off his and say," I don't know if I can handle this. It's ridiculous. I had my first abortion the year you were born. What do you think of that?"

He steps away from me and with one swift motion strips off his jeans and jockeys, showing me a leaping lollapalooza. It was pointing straight at me. I notice his eyes are green as gooseberries. I wonder if he is scared as I am, but he says simply, "I think you are very beautiful and I want to take you to bed."What can I do but grab that sweet worm with my open hand and lead it to my fragrant, leafy nest?

Stromboli

The first time I saw a peacock live was on the island of Stromboli. It was the pet of the old man who owned the pensione in which I had rented a narrow pink room with a cross over the bed. The peacock, as ancient, mottled and disheveled as its owner, flopped listlessly about in the meadow all day. The poor bird never ascended up into the olive groves ringing the volcano behind us, which was still active and steaming and discharging fiery cinders into the sky.

I wanted to ascend the volcano, feel the molten fire flicker inside my thighs, but the old man said the only guide had recently died and the ascent was too dangerous "por una seignorina americaine" like me.

The mythical Siren's song really exists; I heard it on Stromboli. It is the sound the wind makes as it whistles and hisses through the subterranean volcanic caverns beneath the sea. At night, in my pink room, I heard the Sirens song, but their fabled music did not turn me into a pig except for in the metaphorical sense. I started dreaming bestial, sensual dreams. My brother was plunging a wine bottle into me while I sucked desperately at the nipple of a man wearing a goat's mask, a long-bodied man like Steven. Then he was inside me, pounding, hurting me. He pulled out and came on my face, submerging me in sticky, white foam. I struggled to raise myself above the white mess, but when I opened my gummy eyes a bulging scrotal sac, rosy as a ripe persimmon danced before me. I watched horrified as it changed into a grinning death's head. I had arrived at an age where men no longer turned to look at me on the street, yet when I looked into the mirror I could still see my beauty shining behind my eyes like a rainbow outside a dirty window.

After my tryst back in Brooklyn with young but oh-so-sweet Owen, I waited for him to call for two weeks, while entertaining Harold and Maude fantasies. Then despite myself, I started to dream about Steven again. He would invade my sleep, naked, kneeling between my legs, his long thick cock bobbing just above me. He'd grab my hand and put it on him, as in our past life, and then, because he liked me to do it, I would guide him inside me. Just as I could feel him filling me up, I would wake, fingering myself, the sheet beneath me wet with my sweat.

I had already left a dozen messages at least on his answering machine and I had to struggle to keep from calling him again, knew I had to separate from him, get him out of my head, but how? Then one day I found a generous check in my mailbox from Susie Bright. My story, "The Razor," had been accepted for *Best American Erotica 1997*. I decided to use the money to take a trip. I would spend a few weeks in Italy. My friend Irene, a former flight attendant, who married an Italian and visited his family there often, said it was the most romantic country she had ever been to. I hoped I would find the romance there that I needed to help me move on.

I had no luck. The only propositions I got in Rome where from the cabdrivers. Two rock musicians from California did approach me when I was touring the Coliseum. They thought I was Italian because of my long dark hair, they thought I was a passionate, Anna Magnani type, but when they found out I was a Brooklyn girl, they hurried away. One of them said back over his shoulder, "Yeah, now I see, with that nose you are not Italian, you look more like Lucille Ball."

Then I went to Florence. The waiter in the hotel I stayed in, Hotel Bologna, kept propositioning me. His hips were trim and agile beneath his shiny black pants, but his voice was so oily and insincere I imagined he would arise from bedding me and take from the pocket of those shiny pants, which he had thrown casually over a chair, a bill he had already prepared, 25 lire for cunnilingus, plus 150 more por la grande azuine de l'amore.

I left Florence and traveled to Messina, where I took the hydrofoil to Stromboli because a taxi driver in Rome had told me there was an artists' colony there. I had been combing the island for four days and the only people I encountered besides the inhabitants of the island were German tourists, many of them wearing lederhosen despite the equatorial heat.

A dirt road circled the island at the base of the volcano, footpaths diverging here and there to either side. One afternoon I took one of these paths up towards the volcano and found myself in the cemetery. The graves were cut into the side of the volcano like drawers. Photographs were mounted in frames on the outside of each drawer above the name and dates of birth and death of the dead. Some of the photos were so old and weathered that all that remained was a dusty, white page.

There was a one-room church with a wooden cross on the roof and a small store near the pier where the hydrofoil docked each morning. The store stocked canned goods, month-old newspapers from Rome, bread and cheese. I bought bread and cheese to nibble on my walks around the island. In the late afternoon I went down to the beach. Often there were German tourists there, but when I approached them they would not speak to me. In the evenings I sat on the terrazzo of my pensione, where I was the only guest, and ate overcooked spaghetti in a lumpy, tomato sauce, washing it down with musty red wine. The old man sat at a table behind me smoking cigarettes and drinking coffee while the peacock flopped about in the meadow.

How the peacock got to the island was a mystery to me. Maybe Ingrid Bergman left it behind when she was making the film called, appropriately enough, Stromboli, during her torrid romance with Roberto Rossellini. Ingrid Bergman had long been one of my idols, a glamorous movie star who lived the life she wanted to live and loved the men she wanted to love. Alas, though, all three of her husbands divorced her and married much younger women.

On my fifth night on Stromboli, as the Sirens sang their yearning song, I dreamed of strong legs locked around my head, a thick cock thrusting into my aching, tortured mouth. A centaur chased me through the olive groves and trapped me beneath his massive hooves. Just as he reared above me, about to split me in two with his huge pestle, I woke with a start. I reached for the jug of water beside the bed and drank deeply. I went to stand before the narrow window.

The sun was peeking over the top of the volcano, and the last threads of night were fading from the sky. In the dawn light the old man was standing at the center of the meadow; the stained white cotton trousers he wore every day down around his heels. He was holding the peacock by the wings on top of his phallus, and his stringy buttocks moved feverishly to and fro in the dance of desire. High above this tableau of love, the volcano flicked out its fiery tongue.

That afternoon on the beach I met a photographer from Sweden who told me the artists' colony I was seeking was on Panarea, the next island over. As I was eating my spaghetti on the terrazzo that night, the old man came up behind me and put his hands over my breasts. I bolted from the table, ran into my room, locked the door and pushed the bed up against it.

The next morning I took the hydrofoil to Panarea. I found lodgings in another seedy pensione, this one filled with dilettante artists strung out on hashish and heroin. I spent my first night on Panarea with a Russian painter, who gave me a red pill, which he said was mescaline. I passed out immediately. Who knows what it really was? When I came to, he was gone, as were the three travelers checks in my purse. Then I came down with dysentery. I could not leave the bed for two weeks except to go to the toilet. The owner of the pensione brought me a tray of food every day, but I could barely eat. When I recovered, all my clothes were too big, but I was lucky. The Russian painter did not find my remaining traveler's checks, which were stashed in a Tampax box in the bathroom. I decided to resume my travels by going to Amsterdam. I had always dreamed of visiting that fabled city.

A long time ago, the man with the size thirteen feet recommended a hotel there. He had spent a lot of time in Amsterdam. He always stayed at the Hotel Winston on the edge of the notorious red light district. The owners were natives, former Provos, and each room was decorated by a local artist. Rates were reasonable, the complementary breakfast so generous you could eat for a day. From the phone in the lobby of the pensione, I reached Amsterdam information, got the number of the Winston and reserved a room for a week.

Amsterdam

"Desire is the essence of life."
— Benedict Spinoza

It is my first day in Amsterdam. I checked into Hotel Winston on Warmostraddt, downtown at the edge of the red light district. The only "decoration" in my room was a large photograph hanging above the bed, a picture of two fat, hairy gray pigs in black leather harnesses. What a welcome! I tell myself I will get used to the pigs, but I am not convinced. However, I did not come to Amsterdam to stay in my room and look at an ugly picture.

I came to Amsterdam to get stoned, very stoned, so stoned I can grow wings on my feet and believe I will be forever young. I need to find one of the infamous cafes where I can smoke pot and hash legally all day long if I want to. A guidebook and Dutch guilders are already in my bag. I sling it across my shoulder and am down the stairs, out the door, onto the street. I take a left past a couple of stores, Da Skinny, a tattoo parlor, and Spinoza Chocolats, both closed, and proceed down the block to the corner. There, I find just what I am looking for, Blessings Only Café, the name flashing on and off in the windows in green neon below a green marijuana leaf. It, thankfully, is open and even at this early morning hour, half the tables are occupied. A pungent smell I am quite familiar with perfumes the air.

The owner introduces himself as Benedict, he then proceeds to take good care of me. I choose Thai Joystick from the twenty or so offerings on the menu. He rolls a couple of joints with filters and puts them in a plastic bag so stuffed with grass it would cost fifty dollars at least back in New York. He charges me one guilder, which translates to roughly four dollars. He invites me to enjoy a complimentary cup of their Shangri-La tea. He gives me a pack of matches and seats me at a table in front of the window. The man at the next table is puffing a thin cigarette. He wears a priest's collar. He looks me up and down and makes the peace sign. I light up and as I smoke the tension I am carrying inside fades away.

The buzz of conversation in the café sounds like the leaves humming in a tree. Nothing is weighing me down. For the first time in months I feel free, lighter than air, I am helium floating up through the roof into the sky. I am floating high, so high, I am in the Bangkok Mountains, a lush jungle surrounds me. A steep mossy path opens at my feet. I climb up, up, up through sparkling air to the highest mountain peak. I look out past worlds of flowering valleys to an endless purple sea. I don't know how long I float there.

I feel a hand on my shoulder. I open my eyes. Benedict asks, "Are you okay? Dreaming sweet dreams? Can I get you more tea?" It takes me a few moments to find my voice. I say yes to the sweet dreams, no to more tea. The bright sun streaming thorough the windows beckons me. I want to be walking Amsterdam streets. I thank Benedict for his concern.

"Come back soon," he says as I leave.

I get the guidebook out and search for a destination. I see an ad for the Waterlooplein Flea Market. Oldest market in Amsterdam it says. From the antique to the new, we have what you need! Bargaining encouraged! This is it, this where I want to go. According to the map, Warmostraddt runs into Dam Square. If I cut diagonally across it I will find Zandstratt, which, after some blocks, will take me to Waterlooplein.

Dam Square is packed with tourists. They fill the sidewalk cafés, compete for space to take pictures in front of the famous obelisk that is a monument to World War II dead. I find Zandstraddt easily enough and head down the crowded street, passing souvenir stores, art galleries, food stands that sell raw herring, gelato, chunks of Gouda cheese. Gradually the crowd thins out.

A huge man in torn farmer's overalls, a bandana around his neck, stops before me. He is not looking at my face, he is staring at my rather modest bosom. "Would you like to go for a drink?" he asks. "I pay good." Do I look like a prostitute? I am repelled but somehow flattered. Maybe he is drunk, he smells like it. I duck to one side, run around him, keep going down the block. When I look back he is not following. I keep on. It seems to me as though I am traveling in a straight line, but when I pass Rolling Stone Bicycles, a store I passed at least half an hour ago, I know I am lost. I am tired and very thirsty, my throat dry and parched.

In the middle of a block of ramshackle houses, I find a narrow storefront. The sign on the door says BAR, and below it in smaller letters, Amstel, Heineken, Sake. Sake is my favorite drink. The bar is filled with men, all talking so loudly they could be arguing. I don't see another woman in the place. Over the din I hear Roberta Flack singing "Killing Me Softly With His Song." I need a drink badly. I force myself to look straight ahead and push towards the back where there is an empty seat at the end of the bar. I take it. A man is working at a ledger at a table along the wall, probably the owner. The bartender comes over and I order sake, hot. He leaves to fix it and then, it happens, in an instant. I am surrounded by men, men on all sides, like locusts descending.

They bombard me with questions. Am I lost? Am I looking for my husband? Is that a Jewish nose I have? Maybe I am Spanish with my long black hair? One of them grabs my arm. "How much?" he shouts in my face. Suddenly a big hand whizzes past my ear, smacks the jerk across the nose with such force he staggers back, almost falls. Standing beside me is the man who was working at the table. He speaks a few words softly in Dutch and the locusts scurry quickly away.

"Such rudeness, no courtesy," the man says, shaking his head. "They are animals. A lady should be able to come into a bar in Amsterdam and enjoy a drink." He introduces himself and asks my name. I tell him and ask if he owns the bar, he answers no, he is the accountant. Then he asks, "May I join you?" How could I refuse my gallant defender? He orders a sake from the bartender and asks him to put my drink on his tab. I know very soon he is a smart man because he does not ask me any stupid questions like "why are you alone?" Instead he tells me funny stories about Amsterdam politics and the popular rumor the current mayor is a transvestite. At his request the bartender brings out a bowl of peanuts. Two sakes later he says, "It will give me great pleasure if you will have dinner with me tomorrow evening." I accept his invitation.

That is how I met Jahn. He was not the type of man I am usually attracted to. He is overweight with a chubby face and his fingernails are stained with black ink. He was dressed in a light blue tracksuit, I hate tracksuits, with a faded Levi jacket over it. Later, I learned this was his daily uniform. He is also a chain smoker, lighting a new cigarette off the end of the old one. Smoking is a habit I hate even more than I hate tracksuits but I was enjoying his company. He was such a charmer. He didn't want me to get lost again, so he drew a map on a bar napkin showing me how to get back to Dam Square. It didn't even take fifteen minutes.

The next night Jahn picked me up outside the Winston promptly at eight. It was one of his accounts. We went to an Indonesian restaurant a few blocks away, another account of his, so I could sample the famous riistafel. He had brought along a bottle of sake for us to drink. Only when it was nearly empty did he ask, "I hope it is not too personal a question, but what is going on with you? Do you have someone back in America?" I told him I was married but separated. "Do you want to talk about it?" he asked. "Nah," I told him, "I'm having too good a time. What about you? Is there any romance in your life?"

"Only with my son," he says. "He's nine. My wife and I divorced four years ago. She took him back to live in Poland, her home. Last year she ran away to Brazil with a rich plumber. She left my son with the grandmother. I am fighting in the Polish courts to get full custody. It is my dream."

I told him I hoped his dream comes true. "You deserve it," I said. Then we talked about my writing. "I never read books," Jahn told me, "but if you send me one of your books of poems, I will read it from cover to cover."

"It's a promise," I said.

"Music is my love," he went on, "and I am wild for your American jazz, your rhythm and blues, but I hate your Bob Dylan. He can't sing. He sounds like he is dead." Once this would have been the ultimate deal breaker, but I already liked Jahn so much I didn't care.

Out on the street after our dinner, it was colder. I shivered in my light summer dress. Without me saying a word, Jahn pulled his jacket off and draped it over my shoulders. He put his arm around me. I left it there.

We were headed for the Red Light District. I expected poorly lit streets with many dark alleys, but there was nothing furtive or gloomy about this crowded, well-lit boulevard beside a wide canal. We were not the only couple strolling there, nor was the crowd primarily made up of men; there were also women taking in the sights.

The ladies in the windows were every age, shape, size and color and mostly, they were beautiful. "Sometimes the Dutch call the Red Light District *da rosenbusch,* the rose bush," Jahn said. "The ladies come here to work from all over Europe, from Africa, Russia, even South America. We Dutch see no shame in this profession, the government oversees it. It is fair market exchange. I met my wife when she was working here."

We joined a cluster of people gathered in front of a window lit with blue lights. A pretty blond woman was wearing a red cat suit, the chest cut out to display her enormous breasts, her nipples big as saucers. She grinned, stuck out a fat pink tongue, then put her hands on her hips and turned around. A wide circle had been cut from the seat of her pants exposing her puffy, voluminous ass. She bent and used her fingers to open the crack there, showing off the swollen red bud of her anus. She flexed her hips in rhythm to a song only she could hear, while her asshole opened and closed. The audience clapped and cheered. I was surprised, watching her, to feel a pleasurable tingling between my legs, surprised to feel my panties getting wet.

"Are you excited?" Jahn whispered in my ear. He kissed my cheek, my neck. "What do you say then, shall we go back to your room?" His mouth felt like silk on my skin. He was the nicest man I'd met since Steven and I split up. I said yes.

On the way back he kept his arm around me. When we passed Blessings Only Café, it was so crowded I could not see Benedict inside. Jahn knew Benedict too, another of his clients. Both Da Skinny and Spinoza Chocolats were open. Jahn insisted on going inside to buy me a bonbon. I wondered if the owners were descendants of the esteemed Dutch philosopher who lived in the 1600s. More likely they were entrepreneurs capitalizing on his famous name. I chose a green marzipan leaf heavily drizzled with chocolate. We shared it on our way up the stairs.

When Jahn saw the pig picture over my bed, he started laughing, "Not very encouraging," I said. "It's funny, silly," he said. "They gave you the pig room, the least popular room in the hotel. I can have it changed if you want."

"I don't know, m-maybe," I stuttered. I was thinking about something else, I was scared. "Whatever you want, anyhow we do not need encouragement," Jahn said and he opened his arms to me.

I just stood there. I wanted him but I had not been with anyone except Steven for so long. Would I even remember the moves? Jahn must have sensed my anxiety. He didn't get all macho and try to overpower me. Instead he sat down on the bed.

"Come, give us a kiss," he said. "Show me how you like to be kissed." I approached shyly and sat on his lap. I brushed my mouth against his. I licked his lips. His breath smelled like chocolate, marzipan and cigarettes. I kissed him, soft at first then harder. He kissed me back put his arms around me, pulling me so close I could feel his heart beating. I grew bolder, pushing my tongue into his mouth, in and out, fucking him with it. He liked that. I could feel his appreciation grow against my legs.

He lifted me off his lap, put me down flat on my back on the bed and peeled off my clothes. Then he stripped and stood naked before me. I had never been with such a corpulent man, his pendulous belly hung down to just above his crotch. He was uncut, my preference, the foreskin already rolled back to reveal his magnificent erection. He used it to tap, tap, tap my breasts, then he bent his head and started to suck them. He took his time, first one, then the other. He was able to take a whole tit into his mouth. How did he know having my tits sucked drove me wild? Maybe he was the great god Pan and his big belly held all the sex secrets of the centuries. I wanted him inside me. I could barely get my hand around his splendid cock but I managed to guide him into my heart of hearts. He was very sensitive, so practiced he made me come again and again and again, until finally he pulled out and shot between my breasts. He rubbed the creamy stuff all over my skin like a love potion. I was so happy. I curled up in Jahn's arms like a baby and he gathered me onto to his chest. He rocked me back and forth, back and forth, while I sucked his nipples until he was ready to come again.

Jahn had to work during the day, but we spent the next three nights together. We didn't change the room, we decided the pigs were smiling. It was our place. It was where we smoked the hashish we got from Benedict and where we traveled round and round the world.

Jahn also took me sightseeing. We went waterbiking on the canals and twice to the renowned Club Paradiso. One afternoon, following Jahn's directions, I found the Waterlooplein Flea Market and the perfect black leather jacket, a tailored blazer with a Paris label and a stash pocket. I visited Rembrandt's house, which was now also a museum, and the Anne Frank House, which the guard told me was the most popular tourist attraction in Amsterdam.

On our last night together, Jahn gave me a big bottle of Chanel #5 and a pair of white satin crotchless panties. I gave him the best blowjob he ever had, or so he said.

He wanted to skip work the next morning and come with me to Schiphol airport, but I don't like long, sentimental partings and I was afraid I would break down and cry. I did let him walk me to Central Station where I would get the shuttle to the airport.

"Don't forget me," Jahn told me after we kissed goodbye.

"Never," I said.

Athena

My grandparents lived a miracle, a happy married life. We lived with them when I was small. When they were well into their eighties, my grandfather used to chase my grandmother around the house into their bedroom and shut the door. Sometimes they stayed there for hours.

I spent a lot of time with my grandmother in the kitchen. Early on she started to sell me on the virtues of connubial bliss. Chopping up the chicken for soup, she would tell me sex was a baruch, a blessing. Rolling out the crust for a strudel, she predicted that I would love sex as much as she did. I had a little rolling pin that my mother gave me and my own miniature mound of dough so I could practice. I must have been five or so when she started telling me about the pleasures of married love. I listened intently as she told me how babies are made. She told me that when a man and a woman fell in love they got married, then they kissed and hugged and made a baby. For a long time I believed that was all there was to it. Eventually I found out it was not so simple and that you didn't have to be married to have sex or make babies. However, my grandmother's prediction that I would love sex and never get enough has come true a hundred times over at least.

I can't decide if my love of sex has kept me from going completely crazy or driven me so crazy that I can finally see things clearly. I may never spend time with Jahn again but I know I will always have a special place in my heart for him. He reminded me that sex can be caring, comforting, tender and red hot at the same time. Schopenhauer says sex is the will to live. I believe this is true, and I want to have the best sex, the best life I can. I can't have that with Steven, it got too hard, no pun intended. We did have something but we lost it. The real enemy is bitterness. I wish him well but why beat a dead horse? I am going to file for divorce.

Now is the time for me to let go and move on. I tell myself life is full of surprises. Jahn helped me by treating me like I am a goddess. All women are goddesses, although this is often hard to remember in a culture that glorifies Barbie dolls. You are a goddess with a wealth of words at your command, I tell myself again and again.

Yet, despite what Jahn has taught me, despite my resolve to get a divorce, there are too many times since I made the decision that I find myself berserk over the failure of my marriage. I wander back and forth in my two rooms, unable to sit down at the computer and concentrate on my writing. I keep berating myself for the mistakes I made along the way. I try to rally. I know I must go forward so I seek consolation by getting my beloved copy of Robert Graves' *Greek Myths* down from the shelf to read about my favorite goddess, Pallas Athena. She invented the flute, the trumpet, the earthenware pot, the chariot and the ship. Many gods wanted to marry her but she turned them down because she wanted to be free. Although she was the Goddess of War, she got no pleasure from battle, but once engaged in battle, she never lost the day.

One morning I call on Athena to help me and then I drink a hefty shot of gin as I summon the courage to phone Steven and tell him I'm going to file for divorce. He answers the phone on the second ring. His voice is slurred but, "Hello Angel," he says as if he is glad to hear from me. When I tell him I'm going to file for divorce, there is a long pause.

"You can't, you're my wife," he says. This is a surprise; I thought he would be glad I am taking the initiative. He must be drunk or worse.

"I don't want to be your wife anymore, I'm going to file," I tell him. He hangs up.

Obviously, he is not going to co-operate. I will have to find out from the divorce lawyer what grounds for divorce I could use, maybe desertion. After all, he was the one who moved out. I will have to pay for the divorce myself, that much is clear. Maybe it will be expensive; probably I will have to sell my engagement ring to afford it. Maybe that still won't be enough.

I need Athena on my side, I want her to help me. Maybe Athena will lend me her big pot and I will cook up such a potboiler of a novel that it will actually sell. The book will be filled with eccentric, raving madwomen like me. We will all find success in our careers and only after that, true love and happiness. The truth is I could never write a novel. I don't have the attention span, maybe it was all those drugs in the sixties, maybe it is because I find truth more fascinating than fiction. Here is a true story, see if you agree.

The liquor store sends a big, gangly gangsta boy with the eyes of a poet to deliver my nightly bottle of narcotic gin. I ask him to come up to my apartment while I search through my desk drawer for the money to pay him.

"You got a nice place here," he says when he gets inside. Then, he glides up behind me with one big step and starts kissing my neck. He cups my ass with a firm, sure hand and then I wake up on my stomach with my fingers reaching between my legs, wake up wet and alone again. Early morning sun is breaking through the window and the room is filling with light. Lately I find love only in my dreams. Sometimes it's Jahn who visits me, but alas, more often it is Steven and today this cute gangsta boy. I did try recently to get some real life action in my bed. I invited the sculptor who works in the hardware store down the street to come up for a beer. He rejected my invitation. "I'm not attracted to older women," is what he told me. I allow myself the comfort of my bed for a few more minutes, then force myself up, put the coffee water on. I glance out the kitchen window.

There is a long, black hearse parked by the downstairs door. A minute later two men in business suits come out the door carrying a stretcher on which is resting a black body bag. I realize my downstairs neighbor Jim has died. He has been battling lung cancer for three years, a tough old codger from Maine, never a complaint out of him.

He came to New York in the early fifties to be a poet, drove a taxi, ended up making a fortune writing cigarette commercials, lived here forty years, went downstairs thousands of times and today his final descent, feet first. As they open the back door of the hearse and slide the body bag in I can hear that old commercial, "L-S-M-F-T, Lucky Strike means fine tobacco," one of his big hits. It must be Athena on the trumpet, only she could hit those high notes.

The sight of the body bag and the hearse reminds me of the brevity of life, reminds me not to waste time. I go to the phone and call the number Ursula gave me, the number of the lawyer who handled her divorce. His name is Michael McBride and I make an appointment to see him on Friday.

I feel shaky, crazy; the grim reaper has visited in our building and taken my neighbor away. I have a sudden desire to call Steven and beg him to come over and comfort me. Instead I beg Athena for strength, masturbate three times, drink more gin and immerse myself in the *Greek Myths* again. I read about how Athena was also the goddess who inspired oracles and presided over all the arts and maybe that is why I decide to go to a Lower East Side poetry reading that night. A women poet I know is reading in the back room at Max Fish. The audience numbers about fifteen, all women and one man. I recognize him as the consort of one of the women in the audience, a poet who writes about her job as a dominatrix. The man is her slave. He rubs salve on her tricks after a whipping and cleans the mess up when they shit. The featured poet starts to read.

She does a long set with no break, maybe twenty poems, all bitter maledictions against men she has invited into her bed. The audience hoots and claps but all this negativity makes me sick. I want to run out of Max Fish and find another saloon to get sloshed in but I force myself to stay until she is finished. Maybe it is Athena that moves me but to my own surprise I go up to her after she has received all her congratulations and find myself telling her that her fury only chains her, that hatred clouds your thinking, makes her a slave to whom and what you despise.

She stares at me in silence, then sparks fly from her eyes, she snickers. "You're jealous," she says, "you write like Jackie Collins on a bad hair day." She turns back to her adoring fans. She does not know I consider her remark a compliment.

When I get home I do what I always do first thing and check my answering machine. If the red light is blinking on and off it will prove that I am wanted, needed, loved. I know it is pathetic, seeking validation from an answering machine but I wonder how many thousands, maybe millions across the nation are doing it.

There are two messages on the machine, one from my mother asking me to call and one from Steven asking the same. I call my mother. I have not yet told her I am getting a divorce but I have already told her several times that Steven and I are separated, as she was constantly asking to talk to him when she called. This news did not precipitate a stroke as my father and I had feared. Rather, she seemed to rally, she has a new crusade. Now she calls everyday and urges me to reconcile with Steven. I call her back even though I know what she wants to talk about.

"After all," she says to me today, "You are over fifty. In a few more years, who will want you?" I fight back the tears and tell my mother I can take care of myself. I tell her I love her and get off the phone. I forgive my mother everything and very much wish I had talked with her more, spent more time with her before her mind started to wander. Last week, in the middle of a phone conversation about what shade of red she should tint her hair, she suddenly said, "Oh Mildred," her dead sister, "you're so lazy. I always have to make the bed."

I can't understand the message Steven left. I recognize his voice, of course, but the words are so fuzzy and blurred that I don't understand what he is trying to say. I don't have to be a detective to know he is getting into harder drugs. Concerned "friends" keep calling to tell me has been seen nodding out at social events. Last week, when I was driving back from the Right Bank late one night, I saw him milling around in the crowd that is always in front of the Chinese take-out across from the projects. Rumor has it that they sell ten-dollar bags of heroin there as well as fried rice and egg foo young.

I don't want to call Steven back. Instead I call the liquor store and order my usual Tanqueray. I stick a twenty in my jeans pocket so when the delivery guy rings the bell I am ready to go down, get my bottle and pay him. Fifteen minutes later, when the bell rings, I run downstairs and open the door and there is the gangsta boy, my dream gangsta boy.

His huge, dark eyes are sparkling. He smiles at me, says, "Here's your order, Ma'am." For I minute I find myself thinking I will invite him up, show him my big sweet ass as I bend over and pretend to look for money in the drawer of the kitchen cabinet. He will be inflamed with desire and take me in his arms.

There is something about his eyes, they are too bright. I can not see his pupils at all, his eyes are like mirrors glazed over by fog, maybe he just smoked reefer or maybe he took a walk over to the Chinese take-out or maybe what I am seeing reflected in his eyes is the shine of my own desperation. I realize I do not want a pretty boy or a quick fix that will fade tomorrow morning. If I want anything at all, it is a big man who can go the distance. I take the bottle from him and give him the twenty that is in my pocket. "Keep the change," I tell him and then I go back upstairs.

Marrakesh

Last night I did not dream of the gangsta boy or of Jahn or Steven. Instead I had a Marrakesh dream again. I have been having these dreams for five years at least. I started to have them before I even met Steven. They started when my periods became irregular and I entered that bewildering stage in life called in the medical books "pre-menopause."I do not know if the walled city of my dreams in the desert is really Marrakesh, the city of my dreams, but I call it Marrakesh because I love the old Crosby, Stills, Nash and Young song. Since I filed for divorce these Marrakesh dreams have become more frequent. I have them at least once, sometimes twice a week. In the dream, I am walking through the winding streets of the ancient city beneath crumbling, antique buildings with towers and minarets. Beggar boys follow me, their hands outstretched, their eyes filled with questions.

I walk a long way, finally stopping at a corner where the air is filled with the scent of almonds and oranges, the smells of expectancy and promise. Yet, when I turn the corner I come upon a street like all the others: narrow, deep, twisting down into shadows. I wake up and open my eyes. It is still night and empty, cold space surrounds me. I find the covers with my fingers, pull them close around me like the arms of a lover. I want to feel the skin of another being next to mine. I want the heat, the comfort, the dank, earthy abundant smells.

They say that after menopause desire lessens: often the vagina shrinks, becomes a parched, dry tube indifferent as a straw. Then, as Germaine Greer suggests, a woman can become an elder of her tribe, a wise, all-seeing old crone. Others will seek her out with their problems; she can serve them homilies on a plate with sponge cake and cups of chamomile tea. This is supposed to compensate for the banking of the fires, the loss of desire. I do not think this life of a crone would work for me. Lately, despite my irregular periods, my desires, if anything, have intensified. Maybe I am one of the tribe of Ishmael, doomed to be always seeking but never finding.

I refuse to volunteer for charity work as women of my age are urged to do. I would rather search for a buccaneer love pirate in a sordid last-chance saloon than spend my evenings in a soup kitchen in a church basement slicing up humble pie for the hopeless. Sometimes I spend a whole hour anointing my vagina with estrogen creams to keep it supple and receptive, and then perfuming my labia with evening primrose oil. I no longer see my physical body as a jolly toy I play with to give me pleasure. It is now more than that. My body has become more precious with age. I can no longer be casual about sex. I appreciate it more then ever even though I am not as acrobatic as I was or capable of doing it all night and into the next day at one stretch. Now on the rare occasion when I do make love, the experience brings a kind of redemption. In the few moments after orgasm lies a brief peace, the peace beyond understanding.

What was formerly known as sex has become holy and in those moments I'm afraid of nothing, not even getting old, not even death. I fantasize, reclining perfumed and ready on my bed, about the arrival of my next lover, and how his body will fill me, however briefly, with strength. Sometimes I reflect upon my mad past. I can see myself in a clothes closet with a married musician at a party in Hell's Kitchen in the late sixties. My panties are down around my ankles and he lifts me on to him. I can even remember the clothes I was wearing during my past adventures, like the blue polka-dot dress I had on when I was blowing the gas station attendant in the bathroom of a station in Fort Meyers, Florida, to pay for my tank of gas. I am not sorry for any of this, nor am I sorry that time and loss have taught me how holy the body is. I have also learned the hard way how the body of another can be a slate to write one's frustrations on. No one has been able to remove the plum-colored dot on the underside of my left breast where my first husband burned me with a cigarette because I disturbed his sleepy snoring.

Last year in the newspapers I read about a sadist masquerading as a sympathetic top who picked up men and took them back to his plush Park Ave apartment for a night of consensual sex. However, when they got to his place and he had his prey handcuffed to the bed, all promises were forgotten. His victims were raped with wire coat hangers, whipped nearly to death. Is this kind of sex holy? Perhaps only St.

Genet knows how intense physical pain can transform the soul. I suspect that when the pain gets most intense you zone out on endorphins, feel nothing, see a white angel beckoning, waiting to enfold you in feathery arms. I don't know if anyone could survey how many people have been killed in rough sex. The cause of death would probably be listed as a heart attack, but I am sure that on any true list of causes of death, corporate greed would exceed all the rest.

Maybe that is why I keep dreaming of Marrakesh. In my dreams Marrakesh is an ancient place without corporations, satellite dishes or McDonalds. Maybe the reason I dream about Marrakesh is because in my Marrakesh dreams I am always very young, always thirteen, the age of my first menstruation. Because I am Jewish I am free to walk the streets unveiled, my glossy brown hair in a long braid down my back. Men turn to look at me. Some of them make clicking noises in their throats. Once, a tall, bearded man steps out of a doorway to hand me a rose. In another dream a dog was following me, a sleek, yellow hound with startling blue eyes, his hot breath rustling my skirts. We came to an alley strewn with garbage and bits of broken crockery. I thought about going to the back of the alley, kneeling, lifting my skirts, and spreading my legs so he could lick me with his oily tongue, but I didn't have the nerve. Instead I walked faster and faster, I could hear him trotting behind me but when I got to the Fountain of the Caliphs and looked back, he was gone. I woke up wet between the legs, disappointed and forlorn.

Mighty Sampson

It's been more than a month since I saw McBride, the divorce lawyer, three weeks at least since Steven has received the papers. No word yet from McBride that he has received the signed papers back from Steven.

Last week I found out from Al, my bartender friend at the Right Bank, that Steven lost his job and has been picking up what day jobs he can. He is three months behind in the rent for his studio and is nursing the cockeyed idea he can cozy up to me and move back in here.

This news made me feel sick and I drank so much I'm lucky I drove home without an accident.

The next morning in the bathroom mirror the nose ring I got because I thought it would make me look sexy looks cheap and tawdry. The vertical creases above my nose seemed to have grown deeper. I felt so lost, lonely and angry. I want some skin, some warm loving skin against mine. I think seriously about taking out a personal ad. It is not fun being newly single or "NS," as the personal ads say. However, I'm not interested in fine dining, sports, or the outdoors. I don't like cuddling: I prefer a good solid fuck. I'm not solvent, stable, supportive, sincere, respectful or caring, so there is not much chance a shining knight will ride out of the classifieds and save me.

I realized I had to do something, take hold, hone my survival skills, chart a steady course, study Akido or perhaps Tae Kwan Do. Since I am too poor to afford classes, I had to invent my own course of self-improvement or risk being doomed to drift through my life like a rudderless ship. Since I knew exercise helps so many things I decided to take daily long walks just like one my favorite writers, I. B. Singer. He walked five miles a day and lived to be eighty-five. I set myself a goal of five miles a day, and it's been nearly a week that I have stuck to it. Maybe I'm imagining it, but my thighs are already feeling tighter, and my complexion is less gray. I have started to look forward to the late afternoon when, after I've finished my writing, my masturbation rituals, my shoddy pretense at cleaning the house by wiping the kitchen table with a paper towel, I put on my sneakers and head out.

Sometimes I go south through Brooklyn towards Prospect Park; other days I do what I did today and go out my door up Water Street, down New Dock Street, under the BQE underpass, up to the Brooklyn Bridge walkway. As I walk across the bridge, the panorama of the skyline, the view of the Statue of Liberty resolutely holding up her torch, always takes me higher. Once I get to the Manhattan side I may walk through Chinatown or across Canal Street and up through Soho.

I remember the many other times I walked these streets in my earlier incarnations of hippie chick, would-be modern dancer, anti-war activist, promiscuous party girl, neurotic, spasmodic poet. There are moments since I've started these walks I swear I've felt the ghost of one of my earlier selves walking beside me.

Today I walk up Centre St., veer over onto Lafayette, then walk uptown to cross Canal Street. I pass shop after shop selling restaurant equipment and supplies. As I approach a store with a particularly attractive display of soup tureens and crockery, I notice a wooden sign above the high glass door. "Mighty Sampson's Bar," it says in faded gold letters.

Across my mind's eye flashes a picture of Mighty Sampson, Lenny Sandberg from the Bronx. He was my boss when I worked in this now-vanished bar long ago. The year was 1969. I was wearing tie-dye shirts, platform shoes, bell-bottom jeans. It was autumn when I started the job. I remember I had put on my beloved purple, fringed suede jacket when I went to apply for it.

I had just come back from Berkeley where I had gone to see my first ex-husband, thinking we might reconcile. Once I got there, I found out that although he had gotten a Ph.D. in psychology and was wildly experimenting with psychotropic drugs, he was, under his new hip veneer, the same spoiled mama's boy. As Gertrude Stein might say, when you tried to find out who he was, there was no one there.

I was broke and desperately needed a job so I could get on with my life. When I saw the ad in the *Daily News* for "Barmaid, Evenings, Downtown," with the address on Lafayette St., I rushed over.

There was a crudely lettered sign in the window, "2 for 1, 5 to 9." It was early afternoon, and no one was inside, except for a roly-poly fat guy behind the bar and a sweet-faced young man wearing an apron sitting at a back table reading a newspaper. I asked the man behind the bar if he was Mighty Sampson and he said, "Yeah, but you can call me Lenny."

He looked me up and down, and then he smiled, which set his chins jiggling. When he asked if I had experience, I lied and said yes; then he said he liked my style. I could start that night: the pay was two dollars an hour off the books plus tips. I was overjoyed. He introduced the fresh-faced young man as his cousin David. David doubled as short order cook and janitor. Lenny asked David to show me the ropes.

At that time, the neighborhood was full of printing shops, and the bar's clientele was made up of the printers and typesetters who worked on the block. Despite my lack of experience, I got through the night. I kept smiling, poured beers and shots, kept emptying the ashtrays. When Lenny checked out the register after last call, he said I was doing all right.

Over the next few evenings, I got to know David, who was a sweetheart but not too bright. I had to print the food orders in capital letters because he could not read them otherwise. He idolized his cousin Lenny and told me Lenny was getting married next month.

One night during my second week on the job, Lenny wasn't there when I showed up for my shift. David checked me in. Lenny showed up around eight; he was freshly shaved and barbered and wearing a shiny blue suit. I went down the bar to say hello and complimented him on his suit. He rolled his eyes at me and said, "This is my night to howl, doll." He stood with the men at the bar talking and laughing, but whenever I looked up his eyes were on me.

Towards the end of the evening he came up behind me and pushed his heavy body against mine. "How about you and me going for a little ride, doll?" he asked.

"B-b-but you're getting married," I sputtered out.

"That's why I need something steady on the side, doll," he told me, "and it's gonna be you."

"No, it's not," I said.

"Then you're not working here no more," he replied. He took out his wallet, pulled out a twenty and threw it on the bar. "Here's your pay." He yelled out to David, who had been watching the whole sad scene, "Lock up, will ya?" Then he was out the door.

That was the end of my employment at Mighty Sampson's. I am surprised at how vividly I can recall the whole episode. I wonder how much has really changed. In those days sexual harassment was a term you never heard. Now everyone knows what it means and someone like Lenny could be brought up on charges, so I guess that's progress.

When Lenny got rid of me, I could not take legal recourse, but I did have my revenge. After Lenny stormed out the door, David came over and put his arm around me. "I'm sorry," he said. "Stay around tonight," he said, "make your tips." I did feel like storming right out of there, but I realized he was right. Indeed, I was extra genial behind the bar, and poured all my customers second drinks on the house. I made forty dollars in tips, the most I ever made working a shift at Mighty Sampson's. I helped David close up and then I told him I was feeling kind of down and would like company.

It was the week of the St. Gennaro's Festival on Mulberry Street a few blocks away. We strolled over and wandered up and down between the gambling and food concessions. We used my severance pay to buy sausage and pepper hero sandwiches and beer. David used his own money to try to win me a goldfish on the shooting range. He was a terrible shot, but was determined. After he spent six dollars, I convinced him it was the thought that counts. Since he already blew the money I didn't tell him I don't like goldfish anyway.

I invited him back to my place. We walked there over the Brooklyn Bridge holding hands. He was a surprisingly good lover. He didn't say much. He let his hands and mouth do the talking for him. We made love all night long and then fell asleep as the early light was coming in my windows. I knew Lenny would hear about it. I felt like I had got my power back. I was the true Mighty Sampson.

An Easy Life

"Come on, celebrate. It's your birthday. This is a present from me," Roger says as he spills the white powder out of the glassine envelope onto the dresser top.

"What is it?" I ask, thinking it might be the drug-of-choice this election year, China white heroin.

"Blow," he says.

I haven't seen any blow for a long time, maybe since the early-eighties. That was when I used to party with my friend Lynn. We would snort up a few lines together and then go out dancing. I never cared for blow all that much. I didn't like waking up the next day feeling like I had been on a week-long bender. Nonetheless, there it was in front of me, shiny, opalescent, glistening. I did enough of it back then to know I was not allergic.

Why not? Why not get a little buzz on? I thought. This one time won't hurt me. After all, after so much time spent butting my head against the wall, after so many years spent having a nonstop Jones for caffeine, impossible causes, difficult men, and alcohol, I am still breathing, I am still in the game.

Roger parts the coke into rows with a business card. He rolls up a twenty for a straw, and takes a hit. Then he hands the straw to me and I use it. I have forgotten the feeling of that first hit, like a shot of champagne to the brain. I feel eternal, invincible, as full of grace and light as Tinkerbell. "Atta girl, you did that like a pro," Roger says. He does a line and hands the straw back to me.

So it was I spent the night of my fifty-third birthday in a fourth-floor room of the Howard Johnson Motor Lodge on Eighth Avenue and Forty-Eighth Street with a married thirty-nine-year old film editor named Roger who had picked me up at Raoul's.

At the moment Roger penetrated me I thought of my hopefully soon-to-be-ex-husband. As Roger thrust his thing in and out between my legs,

I saw Steven's face. Oh Sweetheart, I said to the image flickering on my brain screen, Oh Sweetheart, where are you now? I was nowhere near coming. Roger shot his load, mercifully, in about three minutes. As soon as he pulled out and rolled off me, I was up and pulling on my clothes.

"Where are you going? What are you doing?" he asked, his voice shrill and angry.

"Gotta go," I said.

Lying naked on top of the sheets with his fat, white belly spilling out on either side of him, he looked like a beached trout. "But we still got blow,' Roger whined. "I paid for the room and we still got some blow left," he said.

"Thanks, but no thanks," I answered. I couldn't help adding, "Save it for your wife." I was out of there quicker than a flash flood, leaving him spluttering on the bed.

Walking down Eighth Avenue just as the sky was beginning to lighten. I wondered if any of the lonely gentlemen on the street would make me an offer. Nothing happened except a boy who looked about eleven walked beside me for half a block whispering, "Loose joints, ecstasy, crack..."

I hailed a taxi. As I rode though the quiet Sunday morning and across the Brooklyn Bridge to my apartment, a line from Walt Whitman kept running through my head; "Those who defile the living are as bad as those who defile the dead."

Steven and I have been separated for six months now. It hasn't been easy. It took me the first few months of separation to learn that lying awake all night, crying hysterically, berating myself, wondering why I could not be a more loving, accepting, shit-eating wife would not dull the pain. Then I tried to embrace my solitude, my misery, maybe the way to keep from getting blown away was to lean into the wind. Then I went to Italy, hoping to find romance there. I did not. A week later, in Amsterdam, I met Jahn. Because of my affair with him, I realized I had to divorce Steven. Upon my return, I filed for divorce. However, I soon returned to my slovenly ways. I didn't bother to make the bed, lounged about in my dirty underwear drinking gin, reading dead philosophers like Sartre and Kierkegaard. Was Kierkegaard the one who says you will not find consciousness by looking at brain cells through a microscope?

Eventually, I realized that I would not find consciousness in the gin bottle either. I forced myself to take hold. I stood in the shower for an hour. I had one clean white T-shirt and one pair of clean black leggings left, so I put them on and went to sit in front of my typewriter. I didn't put any paper in, just sat there praying I would be able to make some sense out of my messy life. I used to think that I was a civilized woman; when invited for dinner I would bring an appropriate wine, maybe bake a fine cake. When Steven and I were together and unable to communicate, my anger grew so great, I thought only with my animal brain. I am ashamed of my cruelty to him and myself, my vicious reactive behavior. I promise myself that I will try to think before reacting but I know that will take a lot of practice.

I put a clean sheet of paper in the typewriter and make myself type "Think before you speak" 100 times. This somehow clears my head and I decide to paint my bedroom, give it a coat of designer white, paint out the many heel marks above my bed that remind me of the nights of pleasure I shared with Steven. It takes me all week long. I finish at six o' clock on the evening of my birthday. I remember that the last time the room was painted was right before I met Steven. My bedroom looks so pristine and white, a brave new world.

I decide I deserve a birthday drink, a margarita. I put on a sleeveless, long, black linen sheath dress and take a taxi to Raoul's. It was there I met Roger, who came over with the original line, "Don't I know you from somewhere?" I should have known better. I have never been lucky with quick fixes.

When I get home from my birthday adventure, I fall asleep fully dressed on the bed. I am awakened by the phone. It's Ursula. "Happy Birthday," she says. "How do you feel?"

"Older but not wiser," I say, and then I tell her about my night out with Roger. She says I have suffered a great loss with the failure of my marriage; it will take time and won't be easy.

"Right," I say. "After all, I never wanted an easy life."

"Yeah," she says," or you wouldn't have become a writer."

I agree. If I wanted an easy life I would have swallowed all the platitudes they gave me like they were valium and then participated in the American dream. Ursula asks if I want to have dinner with her at Thai Café for my birthday. I love the Thai Cafe and say yes. While we are talking, Beast leaps onto my desk and knocks over the antique wooden Buddha my brother gave me last year on my birthday.

Since Steven has left, Beast has broken the VCR, a juice pitcher, a vase, and now this. Both of Buddha's arms are broken off. I despair.

This Buddha is the guardian of my household. I think I know what Beast is trying to tell me, that I have to take care of business in the here and now and put my failed marriage behind me. I tell Ursula I will see her later and get off the phone. I then grab Beast and lock him in the bathroom.

I take a better look at my injured Buddha. Each break is a clean break and with a little Duco Cement Buddha will be whole again. I am relieved. Maybe Beast is just a clumsy cat, but that explanation is too simple. Maybe Buddha was broken to remind me that although life isn't easy, there is such a thing as progress, such a thing as repair.

The Perfect Daughter

My yoga teacher once told me if you say the name of God as you are dying it will go easier for you. He told me how a disciple standing a few feet behind Gandhi distinctly heard Gandhi say "Ram" an instant after the assassin pulled the trigger. How Gandhi fared, as he was crossing over is something we will never know.

Currently, I am an agnostic, mostly leaning towards belief because despite all our intricate cruelties towards each other, love still exists on this earth. Also, I am impressed by Spinoza's argument that it is better to embrace the idea of God and to pray to a God, any God, just in case there is one. So, what name would I say if I was looking death in the face? Jesus? No. Allah? No. Jehovah? No, well, maybe. After all, I was raised to be an observant Jew. Ganesh? Kali? Yoruba? Who knows?

My brother calls to tell me our mother is getting worse. Her blood pressure is going through the roof. She spends a lot of time just staring into space. "Maybe we should pray," I say. "But to whom?" he asks. We both laugh even though we know this existential dilemma is no joke.

Later that day my father telephones. I tell him I'm planning to come down to visit for Thanksgiving. He tells me he is glad, he finds it hard to cope with caring for my mother. He tells me she falls asleep in her chair ten minutes after dinner and when she wakes up the first thing she says is "Is it time to eat?" She wanders around looking for her shoes when she has them on her feet. I don't tell him that I've been doing that for years. He says maybe I can suggest ways to make his role as caregiver easier. I don't tell him I'm not much of a caregiver. I can barely take care of myself and as for Beast, the only time I remember to change his cat litter is when it stinks so much I can smell it when I am in bed. Instead I tell my father I will see if I can find some books about care giving. In the background I hear my mother's voice. "Stop talking about me, Jerry," she says. "Let me talk to her."

"Hello, dear," my mother says, after my father gives her the phone. I tell her I am coming down for Thanksgiving, "Good," she says, "you and Steven can share the driving."

Although I told my mother several times that Steven and I are separated, I finally told her last week that I had filed for divorce. My heart skips a beat, I cannot breathe. I close my agnostic eyes, whisper, "God help me," several times. In an instant, the breathlessness passes. I think briefly about telling her to say God's name as she is dying but I do not. I know it would not go over well although it might summon back her old acerbic self. She might say, "What are you trying to do, bury me?" I gently remind her that Steven and I have been separated for months and I have filed for divorce. "Oh," is all she says, and then I hear my father's voice on the phone. "We have a big problem here. Looking forward to your visit, Duchess," he says, and he gets off the phone.

My earliest memories are of my mother and I living with my father's parents and extended family in Brownsville, Brooklyn. My father was in Europe fighting against Hitler in the holy war to save the Jews. My mother adored me. When I was being toilet trained, she would sit in the bathroom, holding her hands on my knees, and praising me when I pooped. My aunt, uncle and their three kids lived downstairs. Another aunt lived with her husband and family up the block. My third birthday was celebrated with a two-tier chocolate cake baked by my mother. It was shared by forty family members and friends. My Uncle Morton, wearing a Mickey Mouse mask, made balloon animals for the kids.

Shortly after that my father came home. He had been badly injured but the doctors put him back together. I was born just before he went overseas, so I had never actually seen him before, although I had been shown pictures. When we were introduced, I didn't believe he was my father. In those pictures the man was smiling, and looked nothing like this skinny man with a sad face standing before me.

I could no longer share the big double bed in the back bedroom with my mother. My father took my place. A little bed for me was put in my grandparent's room. My mother still tucked me in at night, but how I missed sleeping beside her. She was always occupied with my father. He spent many months in bed and she sat beside him all day, reading him the newspapers and giving him rubdowns. She did get me a set of miniature cooking utensils and I spent a lot of time in the kitchen with my grandma helping her cook. I still make some of her recipes, especially the cherry noodle pudding, which I bring to parties.

Eventually, my mother nursed my father back to health. He took a job with the Census Bureau and traveled by subway to his office in the Bronx every morning. When he came home from work in the evenings, she buzzed around him, sitting with him in the living room while they drank pre-dinner rum and cokes. My mother and I were rarely alone. She still praised me for being a good girl and called me her perfect daughter, but it was not enough.

When I was eight, my baby brother came along. Our little family moved into a home of our own, a four-room apartment in a new housing project in Sheepshead Bay. My brother was sickly and always crying. One day, when he was a few months old, I took him out of his crib and dropped him on the floor. He started to cry like his head was cracked open. My mother rushed in, she had been cleaning the bathroom.

"How did he get on the floor? What happened?" she wanted to know as she picked him up and rocked him in her arms.

I told her, "I took him out of the crib and dropped him."

"No, no," she answered, a funny smile pulled tight across her face, "you would never do anything like that."

I started to have problems in school. The other kids didn't like me and wouldn't play with me. They called me teacher's pet and goody-goody because I was so desperate for attention I was the one who always raised my hand first. Even worse, I always had the right answer. I never told my mother that I had become the class scapegoat. Such things could not happen to me, the perfect daughter.

As my brother grew older, he became more hyperactive. My mother couldn't keep up with him. She didn't have time for me during the day, but still she stayed up late at night sewing me beautiful clothes. My father wasn't always home in the evenings. I heard my mother tell her sister Mildred on the telephone that he was running around. I didn't know at the time what running around meant. I only knew that my mother looked exhausted and never smiled. She developed a new sharpness. When, in fourth grade, I brought home a report card with all "ninety-eights" she handed it back to me. "What happened to the other two points?" she said.

After school, I started to go straight to the public library branch on Nostrand Avenue, a few blocks from the projects. I would do my homework and then read until it was time to go home for supper. I was reading my way through the young adult fiction section, though I was only ten. I was finally making friends; Sherlock Holmes, Marybeth and

Jo, Anne of Green Gables, Alice Through The Looking Glass, Huck and Jim, Natty Bumpo.

My father got involved with a divorcee who lived in our building. My mother told my grandfather. He stepped in and gave my father hell. Years later, my Aunt Sadie told me the story because she was listening in the next room.

"You make a bargain and then you stick to it," my grandfather told my father, "that is what a marriage is." Then he smacked him so hard my father fell down. My aunt heard the smack and then she heard the thud. My grandfather told my father he had to make a fresh start with his family. He gave us ten thousand dollars so we could move away from the projects and have the down payment for a house.

My parents found a split-level house in Canarsie, in a new development called Seaview Village. For the first time my brother and I had separate bedrooms. My mother worked hard fixing up the new home. She sewed curtains, slipcovers, bedspreads. She cooked all of my father's favorite dinners, but when we sat down to eat, he read the newspapers, gobbled his food. Within six months he was involved with a woman named Hortense. They had dated in high school and then ran into each other again twenty years later at the racetrack. Late at night, when he came home, my parents had screaming fights. I don't know why my mother didn't tell grandpa: maybe it was too difficult for her to admit that, although she made a new try, she was still unable to hold him; maybe the only hope that sustained her was that someday she might win him back.

Eventually the fights stopped. My father still came in late. When he was home, they rarely spoke. My mother started a sewing business in our finished basement. It was so successful she was able to send my brother and me to summer camp. She bought me a red leather jacket, a portable typewriter, a pink electric shaver for the new dark fuzz growing on my legs. When I came home from school, she asked me how my day went. "Okay," was all I ever said. I could not warm up to her. Maybe I was afraid that, if I let her in, she would abandon me again.

I had a new friend, Eleanor. She lived around the corner. She was a year ahead of me but we rode the same bus to Tilden High, a school we both hated. Her parents were Communists who served wine at dinner and always filled my glass when I stayed there for dinner. Every chance we could get, Eleanor and I rode the L train in from Canarsie to Greenwich Village. We made straight for Washington Square Park, where we would buy loose joints, three for five dollars. My father continued to see Hortense. My mother spent her evenings sewing in the basement. She got my brother a telescope; he was fascinated by the stars. He wanted to walk on the moon. He calmed down, started to study, did better in school.

When I was eighteen, I left home and moved into a fourth-floor walk-up on McDougal Street. The rent was thirty-two dollars a month. I got a job and worked my way through Brooklyn College, but that is another story.

Three years after I graduated, the company my father worked for moved to D.C. My parents sold the Canarsie house and bought a condo in suburban Maryland. My father left Hortense behind after the move and my parents somehow reconciled. As far as I know, my father never had another mistress.

He did, however, go in on a racehorse named Molly Malone with some of his new poker buddies. My mother often went with him to watch Molly run at early morning practice. My mother learned to drive; my father taught her. At the age of fifty-six she got her license, passing the test the first time. She got a job in a local mall working in the alterations department of a big department store. Within six months she was the manager of the department and supervised five other seamstresses.

This was a golden time for my mother. She loved her new job and used her employee discount to buy herself expensive shoes and elegant leather pocketbooks. On her days off she combed flea markets to find and buy the fine rose medallion china she loved. She sent me a stunning formal long black dress coat that she bought with her discount, enclosing a note that said "you can use this when you go to the opera and the theater." I didn't have the heart to tell her I never went to the opera or the theater.

My mother knew I had boyfriends and was aware of my bohemian lifestyle, but she didn't pry, I thought she probably didn't want to know. One day she called me on the phone to tell me she and my father were leaving me their condo, so that no matter what, I would always have a home. I told her I would probably sell it. I could not imagine myself living in suburban Maryland. "At least it will be your security," she said.

A few years before my mother got sick, I was visiting. One evening after dinner I was helping her with the dishes. She washed, I dried. Suddenly she turned the faucet off and put down the sponge. She turned to me and said, "If I had known what I know now when you were growing up, things would have been a lot different. I'm so sorry." I continued drying the plate I was holding as if I hadn't heard her. Maybe I was surprised speechless by this unexpected statement, maybe I was shutting her out in the way she used to shut me out whenever I tried to show her how vulnerable and needy I was. I said nothing and the silence hung like a black curtain between us.

Finally, my mother turned the faucet back on, and went back to the dishes. Her shoulders were shaking. She and I could have nourished a new love and understanding. She gave me the chance and I slammed the door in her face. When she first got the Alzheimers diagnosis I tried to re-open the long-ago conversation in the kitchen, but it was too late. She turned away. She said she had to go water her plants.

Now when I go down to Maryland to visit, I hug her and kiss her, sit with my arm around her. Sometimes she doesn't even know me, she calls me Mildred or Irene after her other sister who also has Alzheimers. I don't feel like a perfect daughter, I feel like a disgrace.

Shortly before my mother got sick, she asked me if I would burn a yahrzeit candle for her after she was dead. In the Jewish faith, this is the candle that is burned by family members once a year on the anniversary of the death of the loved one. Maybe she had a premonition of what was coming, I can't ever know but at least I told her yes. My mother believes in the Jewish god. He is the one she started with. She always wore a Jewish star around her neck. My mother was a very loyal person as her continued devotion to my father, and as her attempts to win me back prove.

My mother tried her best in difficult circumstances. She was tough and strong and somehow pulled our family through. Even in the worst of times, she cooked, cleaned and sewed for us. She maintained a lovely home. She was gracious to everyone she met. She always wore lipstick and put her best forward. In this I try to follow her example, although I do not always succeed. While she always voted democratic, she believed in the ideal of democracy; that each person has a right to his or her own opinion. No matter what was going on in our household when I was little, she found a baby sitter on Election Day and went to help out at the polls. Once they moved to Maryland, she convinced my father to do the same thing. This is the first year since she was eighteen and started to vote that she has not been well enough to work at the polling place on Election Day.

I know it will only get harder for her. In the days to come, she will need all the help, all the prayers she can get. I am going to start praying for her soul right now. I do not know if Jehovah exists, but I still will pray to him for my mother because he is her God. What I do know is that my mother is the God who gave me life, at least in the experiential sense. Let Aleister Crowley, the Pope, Kant and Jean Paul Sartre debate the rest.

I hope that Jehovah will listen to me since I have pierced ears, body piercings and a few months ago I pierced my nose. Piercings, like tattoos, are against Jewish law. I have had sex while menstruating (against Jewish law) and behaved like Jezebel and fornicated with many men (against Jewish law). Still I want to believe that any god worth his or her salt would listen to a hopeless sinner like me.

Here is my prayer for my mother. Dear Jehovah, Please help my mother in the trials she will have to face. Please make it easier for her. When the time comes for her to cross over, please help her to do that with the strength and grace with which she has lived her life. Amen.

St. Huncke

Every Spring, Cafe Nico on Ave. A sponsors an evening when venerated beat icon Herbert Huncke reads from his book, *Guilty of Everything,* as well as other new work he may have. All proceedings from these readings go directly to Huncke. The readings are always advertised as "St. Huncke Reads." There are some who might say to call a man who is a junkie, a liar, a hustler and a thief, a saint is pure blasphemy. There are others like me who would rather pray to Herbert Huncke then to a masochistic saint like Saint Theresa, who made a career out of suffering and being pierced by arrows.

I never went to any of the St. Huncke readings because I didn't want to spend the fifteen bucks it took to get in but I did eventually get to meet him. Even before that, however, I saw him in the flesh. It was early one winter morning around one a.m. in the Odessa. I was with my friends David H. and Damian Dread after a poetry reading. We were eating blintzes and reviewing the evening when the street door opened and a slight, wraith-like figure in a long, dark overcoat entered. He moved past our table and into the bathroom at the rear of the restaurant so quickly I didn't get a glimpse of his face. "Herbert Huncke" said Damian, "Yeah, that's him," said David.

I knew about Huncke from reading *On the Road* and *Naked Lunch* and wanted to get a better look at the famous junkie hipster, so I kept an eye on the bathroom. By the time Huncke opened the door again there were four impatient people squirming in their pants lined up outside. Huncke's face was all leathery and worn like an old boot. He exited with a huge smile totally impervious to the dirty looks he was getting from the people waiting to use the loo. As he passed our table he noticed me looking at him. He paused, nodded at me,"Good evening" he said in impeccable diction like he was Lawrence Olivier. His smile so filled his face with light that for an instant I could imagine him as a young boy, a happy-go-lucky gamine. He glided past our table and out the door of the restaurant. "Bet he didn't come in here to take a crap," David said.

A year later I heard Huncke was going to give a reading at the Right Bank Bar and I circled the date on my calendar. When I got there that evening it was crowded with people I had never seen in there before. There were women sporting facial piercings, wearing layers of black clothing and black lipstick, men with pony tails, also wearing black clothing, and sporting facial piercings. Amid this crowd of strangers I spotted Larry King, one of my Right Bank regular buddies, sitting at the bar. There was an empty stool next to him, I went over and sat down.

"Hi, quite the crowd," I said, "makes me want to get my nose pierced." Larry laughed,

"Don't do that," he said. "Whatever you do, don't call attention to that nose." My nose does resemble Barbara Streisand's but is smaller and goes well with my high cheekbones and big eyes. "If you're going to tease my nose," I told Larry, "'the least you can do buy me a drink. " "How about a Spaten beer?" asked Larry, "since it looks like we are in Berlin." "Fine," I answered.

A few minutes later Huncke swept in the door wearing the same long, dark overcoat he had on in the Odessa, even though it was now May. Close behind him like a shadow was a striking, dark-haired man with huge, glistening dark eyes. He was also wearing a long, dark overcoat. As he walked past me towards the stage and chairs set up in the back of the bar, he paused right behind me. He seemed to be admiring my ass. He leaned closer, winked at me, "Hubba-hubba," he said and glided on.

Kerry Smith, the owner of the Right Bank, shook Huncke's hand and led him to the stage. The crowd moved to the back of the bar and took seats. By the time I got there all the chairs had been filled so I leaned against the wall. Leaning against the opposite wall was Huncke's dark-eyed companion. He kept eyeing my body. I caught him licking his lips. He smiled, gave a little wave. I am a sucker for the direct approach, besides he looked so striking, so intelligent. He seemed to give off a magnetic energy. I smiled back.

Huncke was now standing behind the podium. Kerry introduced him to tumultuous applause. "Thank you," Hunke said. He then opened the book he had been holding in his hand, set it on the podium and began to read.

He took us to back to 1943, to the Bucket of Blood Saloon on 8th Ave. and 42nd St.

Suddenly it was as if the whole room was filled with smoke — the overhead fluorescent light filtering through it gave the place an eerie quality. The shouting and talking deafened one and, mixed with the blaring sounds of music, the general atmosphere was like a small slice of hell.

Huncke read for maybe twenty minutes, describing how he was approached by a hustler named Eddie and the adventure that ensued. At the point where Eddie and Huncke had taken a hotel room and Eddie had just tied Hucke off and was ready to shoot him up Huncke stopped reading, leaving his totally enthralled audience hanging on the edge of the needle. He closed the book.

"We will now have a ten-minute intermission," he announced. "You can freshen your drinks, and purchase books at the book table. I will be happy to autograph them." I wanted to buy the book, but before I could make a move, my dark-eyed admirer was standing right in front of me. He seemed to have crossed the floor in a giant leap. He extended his hand, "My name is Louis Cartwright. What is your name, beauty?" I told him my name.

"Did you enjoy what you just heard," he asked. "What do you think?" was my answer, "How could I not? I'm going over right now to buy the book."

"Herbert is a spellbinder," he said. "I am his close friend and companion as well as a world-famous photographer. We have been room mates for twenty-five years. Let me take you over and introduce you, then let me buy you a drink." My hand was still resting in his. I liked how that felt. "Sure," I said. He led me to the book table. Herbert was busy signing. Louis grabbed a book and pulled me to beginning of the line. As soon as Herbert's hands were free, Louis handed him the book. "This is my future wife, Herbert" he said, "She's a precious gem."

That's nice, Louis," Huncke said, then he wrote in the book and handed it to me. He leaned close and whispered into my ear. "My compliments, enjoy the book but you can't believe anything Louis says, my dear," then he turned to the next customer.

Louis led me to the bar, bought us both drinks and we went to stand against the wall with our drinks. He put an arm around me. "You are so intoxicating, I have to lean on you or else I'll fall."

"Who are you, Mr. Cornball?" I said, but I let him keep his arm around me.

Huncke continued where he left off, reading about how he and Eddie became business partners. First they went to Brooklyn, using the phone book, going from doctor to doctor, trying to con morphine prescriptions. They were glib talkers and often succeeded by telling intricate stories describing injuries they never had. They would then fill the prescriptions in Brooklyn where prices were cheaper than in Manhattan. They took the subway back into Times Square and peddled the dope to the hookers working there. They would make ten, maybe fifteen times what they paid for it. Huncke closed the reading with a section describing how he and Eddie went shopping at Abercrombie and Fitch for sporty new clothes. They had made so much money they were planning a trip to California.

Before Herbert and Louis left, Louis asked me for my phone number, "You are my precious gem," he said. "Please let me see you again, your eyes make me so happy. I will call you Esmeralda because of your emerald green eyes."

"My eyes are brown," I told him, but I gave him my phone number.

It wasn't until I got home that I looked at the inscription in the book. On the title page, Herbert had written, "Tsaurah, Know Happiness Always until you weary – this from myself, Herbert Huncke," then right below, he had added, "Whatever you do, don't trust Louis."

Still, when Louis called the next day and invited me to meet him in Tompkins Square Park for a chat and then we would go for drinks, I said yes.

In the park, he regaled me with stories about the exploits he and Huncke had shared. We split a Hershey bar with almonds that he had brought for refreshments. As the sun was setting he suggested we go for a cocktail at Life Café on Avenue B. Outside the door of the café he suddenly grabbed me and kissed me with such passion my knees began to shake. As we disengaged I saw a line of black dots at the base of his neck. I knew they were tracks. I pulled away horrified, turned, started to run away. He was stunned for a minute, then he gave chase, "Esmeralda," he called out, "Where are you going?"

I darted into the open door of a bodega. I brought a few things so the proprietor wouldn't think I was a crazy. I knew I had to go out, tell Louis I could not see him again, but when I stepped fearfully outside he was gone. He called me that night and spoke as if the whole incident had never happened. He said he wanted to buy me a diamond ring. I hung up on him.

The next day, I called my friend David, told him about my date with Louis.

"You would have to be nuts to get involved that guy," David said. "He's been a junkie for thirty years. He would rob his grandmother to get high. Maybe Huncke has some ethics left, he is one of those old time thieves with a code of honor, but that Louis, he's a joker, a wild card. Stay away." I knew David was right.

Louis kept calling me. I told him I wouldn't get involved with anyone doing drugs. "Please, Esmeralda, please," he begged. "No," I said, "no, you would have to have prove that you are clean, at least two negative AIDS tests before I will even consider meeting you for coffee." He said he had twenty-two negative AIDS tests and he would be right over. He called me his true love, said his heart would always be mine. No matter how many times I hung up on him, he kept calling. I was very glad I had never given him my address. Several times, Huncke took the phone out of his hand and said, "You are doing the right thing, my dear. You mustn't believe anything Louis tells you. He is prone to fall in love at first sight and this time I am afraid you are the victim of his affections." Then, suddenly the phone calls stopped.

I heard through the grapevine that he and Huncke had a falling out involving a woman Louis had been pimping out of the apartment off Avenue D. the two of them shared. Louis stormed out of their apartment vowing to never return.

One summer night I saw Louis in Tomkins Square Park with a gang of teen runaways. We spoke briefly; our conversation left me incredibly sad. A month later I got a call from Herbert. "Have you heard from Louis, my dear ?" he asked. "Has he tried to contact you? He was sleeping in the park, friends who were passing through used to see him there, but he's been gone. No one has seen him for weeks. If you hear from him, please tell him all is forgiven." I told Herbert I had seen him there once, but had no contact with him since, but of course I would let him know if I did hear from Louis. Then he said, "So sorry to have disturbed you, my dear. Jack Micheline tells me you're a good writer. Don't let a man, any man, or anything else get in your way. Keep shining."

I never did hear from Louis or Herbert after that. One day, David phoned me. The news was going around that Louis was found murdered in the park along the East River Drive. His throat was slashed.

I have read *Guilty of Everything* several times. I would recommend it to anyone who has a taste for a writer who is outrageous, brilliant and the ultimate Beat storyteller.

Huncke ends *Guilty of Everything* like this: "I don't see anything clearly except that I believe somehow underneath it all there's something that is good. I would like to see man find his niche in the scheme of things. Maybe he has found it — maybe this is the way it should be. Maybe all of this confusion is necessary. Something good may come out of it, but I guess we won't know about it. Perhaps this will all explode and enrich some other planet somewhere else. I don't think anything is wasted, that much I do believe. But in the meantime we try to get by the best we can."

One morning, last year, in the Spring, my friend Annette Planet called me up. "Huncke died," she said, "The obituary is in the *Times*." I got the *Times* and read how Huncke had spent the final two years of his life in the Chelsea Hotel cared for by friends. The last line of the obituary read "Huncke's long time companion Louis Cartwright was murdered in 1994." During our limited acquaintance Herbert Huncke was a consummate gentleman. He always gave me good counsel. Wherever he and that rogue Louis may be out there in the great hereafter, may they rest in peace.

Awakenings Gallery

I wake up with a terrible hangover, jackhammers pounding in my head. The empty gin bottle is sitting on my bedside table next to the empty wine bottle from the night before. When I sit up in bed I see the landscape of my life, laundry basket overflowing, clothes spilled out across the floor, books pulled from the bookcases, left open in piles on the computer table, the dresser.

I get up and stagger into the kitchen towards the bathroom. I relieve myself in the commode, which needs cleaning big time. Out in the kitchen again, I see the sink piled with dishes; dirty pots and pans are on the floor. Everywhere I look there is chaos. I need to escape. I need clear space around me, fresh air.

I decide to go for a walk across the Brooklyn Bridge; maybe that will clear my head. I promise myself I will walk across the Brooklyn Bridge and back again. The wind rattles against the loose pane of glass in the window. It is a brisk November day. I dress, put on my down jacket to keep me warm.

I make it to the bridge entrance three blocks from my building. I'm already tired, that's what the gin diet does for me, wears me out. I don't know what time it is, but judging from the position of the sun in the sky, it's not yet noon. There are few people on the bridge to see my unkempt hair, my unsteady gait. Shaking from the booze, I collapse on a bench at the midpoint of the wooden walkway. I have to face it; I'm becoming a drunk. I already am a drunk. How did this happen? Did it start with that first glass of wine I poured to keep me company at dinner a few days after Steven split? I don't know. All I know is I am a drunk and being a drunk is trouble. I start to cry and I can't stop. I cry for my wrecked marriage and all my failed romances. I cry because I keep trying to play the game but I can't learn the rules. I cry because I will never be a girl again. I cry because Steven still hasn't signed the divorce papers I filed three months ago and I feel like a fish twisting on a hook.

As I am crying, in a stunning demonstration of synchronicity, a homeboy in a red hooded sweatshirt pauses as he walks by and says, "Forget it, little mama, the stud ain't worth it." Two Japanese women in mink coats snap my picture. I keep crying until I have no tears left. I just sit there. I smell salt in the air; the East River is not really a river but an estuary of the Atlantic Ocean. My head is still throbbing but it's not as bad as it was. I'm hungry. I want orange juice, I want a whole wheat bagel with cream cheese. I want a better life. I have to stop drinking or I won't have a chance. I'll start today. I'll go home and clean up my place, throw the garbage out.

On the way, I stop in the deli around the corner. I have a five-dollar bill in my pocket, enough for two gallons of Tropicana. I get back to my apartment to find the little red light on my answering machine blinking twice. This makes me feel better, as if two phone calls proves I am a functioning person, part of the larger world. I hit the button to listen to my messages. A whining, plaintive male voice I do not recognize says, "Suzy, pick up your phone. Why don't you pick up your phone?" Wrong number.

The second call is from Steven. He tells my answering machine that he has signed the papers and sent them back to the lawyer. He says his new girlfriends have convinced him it's time to move on. He says his life is going great. He will be part of a group show opening Friday at the Awakenings Gallery in Tribeca. There is no reason we can't at least be friendly, he says. He has no hard feelings, why don't you stop in at the gallery for the opening. He ends his call by saying, "I hope you can come Friday."

I'm amazed at this miraculous transformation, but suspicious too. I wonder if he really has signed the papers, maybe he was stoned when he called me. I call McBride, the divorce lawyer, and when his secretary puts me through to him, I tell him about Steven's call. McBride says he hasn't got the papers yet but reminds me the mails are often crazy. He urges me to be patient. After we get off the phone I feel down in the dumps and I immediately want a drink. Then it occurs to me what a hypocrite I am, wondering if Steven was stoned when he called, when I have become a drunk who wants to drown her frustrations in gin. I remember John Cheever writing about how his need for love and his need for drink were irrevocably entwined. I suspect my need for love and my need for drink are Siamese twins. I force myself to pour myself a large orange juice and drink it down. Then I make myself drink a second glass of juice.

I turn on the TV for company and start to clean. By the time the evening news goes on there are three big plastic bags of garbage out in the hall. I keep on cleaning and when I finish Law and Order is over. I'm so exhausted I fall into bed and immediately sleep.

When I wake up I realize I have finished my first day of sobriety. I'm so hungry, yesterday I forgot to eat. I go to the Gristede's and buy bagels, cream cheese and for a special treat, an Entemann's chocolate cake.

Back home again I eat two bagels with cream cheese. I start working on my on-going novel, Journal of a Masochist Yearning to Be Free. Then my nose starts to bleed. I staunch the flow and as soon as I sit down at the computer, I get diarrhea. When that is over my nose starts to bleed again. I spend the afternoon and evening discharging toxins from both ends. I feel two pounds lighter by the time it ends. Once again, I'm hungry, so I eat the whole Entemann's cake.

The next day I'm woken up by a phone call from the lawyer. He tells me he has received the signed papers from Steven. I'm a step closer to beginning my new life! I'm also immensely relieved Steven wasn't lying to me. Steven's message is still on my answering machine. I can't resist listening to it again.

His voice is steady, not slurred and fuzzy like it gets when he is drugging. I wonder if we could actually be "friendly," and salvage something from our relationship. At least, maybe we should try. I have to also admit that I am curious about these mysterious girlfriends. Will he bring one of them to the opening? I call Steven and leave a message on his machine that I will do my best to make the opening.

For the next few days I drink only orange juice and stay off the booze. When I look at myself in the mirror Friday morning, my eyes are clear and my complexion so rosy I look like a farm girl. I put on my red rubber skirt, a black velour turtleneck, black fishnets and my black cowboy boots. I top this outfit with my long, black leather coat. I'm trying for an elegant-but-hot look and maybe I have succeeded because as soon as I walk into the gallery a man wearing a furry black hat says, "Okay, she's here, now the party can begin."

The gallery is on the ground floor of a factory building. It's crowded and I am surrounded by people with paper cups in their hands. Only weeks ago, I would have made an immediate beeline for the drink table but instead I make myself look at the art. One artist has hung a wooden chair from the wall and draped it in ripped pairs of panty hose. Next to this construction are two small canvasses of identical size. Short brown hairs are pasted over the surface of each. The caption beneath the first one reads, "Monkey's Ass", the caption beneath the second reads, "Donkey's Ass." I can see no difference between them, maybe that's the idea.

Then I see Steven. He is seated next to a standing sculpture he made when we were together, "Bird in Flight?" made from old car tires.

In one hand he holds a paper cup, in the other hand he holds a half-empty bottle of Dewar's. An artist is certainly entitled to get drunk at his opening. His face is flushed in a way I know means he has made a good start. Three women are clustered around him. I step closer and move into his line of vision. He sees me, yells my name and then, "Come over, come over." He announces to the room in general, "Thish is my wife," then he sinks back into his chair. I go over and he introduces me to the women. He tells me their names are Tamara, Nina and Karma. "Thish is my wife," he adds again. The women look distressed, maybe they didn't know there even was a wife. I quickly interject, "soon to be ex-wife. All the papers have been signed." They don't look relieved; maybe they are as drunk as he is. They look so much alike, I wonder if they are triplets. They also have identical silver nose rings and are wearing silver quilted jackets. I am tempted to ask him if Tamara, Nina and Karma are his new love slaves. Instead I say, "Pleased to meet you," and comment on the nice turnout for the show.

The man in the furry hat who greeted me when I entered the gallery materializes at my elbow. "I love your skirt," he says and introduces himself as Sasha, the owner of the gallery. "Is your skirt really rubber?" he asks.

"Yes," I say.

"How daring," he says, "What is your sign?"

I lie as I often do and say, "I'm a triple Scorpio."

"Aha, that's the only sign that excites me," he says. I know he too is lying. He asks me if I would like something to drink and I say, "Yes, a Coke if you have soda, otherwise water."

"What, no wine?" he asks. I pretend I am a dominatrix and he is my slave. I visualize him polishing my toilet with his tongue. "Just bring me a Coke, no ice." I say sternly, "Hurry up. Are you deaf?" He scuttles off to get my drink. I walk away to look at the art. Some witty artist has taped a wire coat hanger to the wall and titled it "Homage to Roe vs. Wade."

A woman comes to stand beside me. "What a surprise to see you," she says, "I didn't know you and Steven were speaking. Are you still getting divorced?" I remember her from my former life with Steven as Barbie, the wife of an art dealer, Gregory, twenty years her senior.

At openings, she used to greet Steven by pressing her hefty breasts, probably a boob job, against his arm at the same time she shook his hand. My personal life is certainly none of her business. "Do you like Steven's piece?" I ask.

She ignores my question, saying instead, "You have lipstick all over your teeth," her voice so saccharine I'm surprised she is not covered with flies. I say nothing and turn back to "Homage to Roe vs. Wade." I give it my full attention until she gets the idea and walks away.

Sasha returns with my Coke."Do I have any lipstick on my teeth?" I ask Sasha and I smile at him.

"Why, no, not at all," he replies.

I let Sasha lead me around. He stops before each piece to tell me something about the artist, then he introduces me to Jacques, a painter from France. Sasha goes off to greet some new arrivals. Jacques and I chat for awhile. He asks me if I live with someone and when I tell him I live alone, he asks me my sign.

"A triple Scorpio," I lie again.

"Ah, I knew it," he says.

I finish my Coke, go to the drink table to get another. I dip a chip into the babaganoosh and turn to survey the gallery. The room has cleared out a bit. Steven is still seated on his chair, but now Barbie is on his lap. She has one arm around his neck. Her other hand is inside his shirt, that fine blue silk shirt I gave him. She is tonguing his ear. He appears to be passed out, or maybe he is overcome with passion. He is drooling and his chin is wet. I can see nothing in him to love. I just feel heavy with sadness to see him so wrecked.

Tamara, Nina, and Karma are standing a few feet away. Karma and Nina are crying, Tamara standing rigidly staring into space beside them. Barbie suddenly stops, raises her head, looks around the room until her eyes find mine. She smiles and goes back to nuzzling his ear. There was a time when I would have wanted to grab her by the ears, throw her down on the floor, stomp her till she is flat as a pancake, but now I don't have the energy. Who cares what she does? I have a life to live. I wonder if I'm thinking like this because I'm not drunk enough, in fact I'm not drunk at all.

Crazy scenes from my drunken past flash before my eyes: the time I climbed up the fire escape to look in Tim's window, the time I kicked down Michael's door after he didn't answer my repeated knocking because I thought he was inside with Linda. I don't need any more psychodrama in my life. It's just too much trouble. This must be what people mean when they talk about the wisdom of sobriety.

I button up my coat, head for the door.

"Must you go?" asks Sasha.

"Oh yes," I say. "Besides, I'm not a Scorpio. I'm really a Virgo."

His mouth falls open, but no words come out. I sail past Tamara and Nina and Karma, who are still crying. Steven is now snoring so loudly I can hear him, Barbie continues to go at him.

Out on the street, the night air is fresh, crisp, and cold. The sky is so clear I can even see a couple of stars. On my way back to where I've parked the car, I see an open deli. I go in and buy a gallon of Tropicana to take home.

Flasher

I have not seen Beast for several days. I asked the neighbors if they had seen him in the halls; perhaps he escaped sometime when I left the door open. After all, in my current state, who would want to room with me, not even a cat, but no one has seen him. I suddenly feel frantic. My feline friend has never deserted me before.

Even though I am waiting for my divorce decree to become final, even though I know from seeing him at that opening what a mess Steven is, I, to my disgust, think of calling Steven to tell him Beast is missing. How crazy is that? Maybe he will offer to come over, help me search the vast basement of the building. I will greet him at the door wearing nothing but my long black leather coat and my black thigh-high boots. I will throw open the door and open my coat. I will flash him. He will be overcome by my naked splendor, step inside, make love to me on the kitchen floor. Hundred dollar bills will rain from the sky and China will free all political prisoners.

This morning I woke up from a dream that a man wearing a Zorro mask was inside me, on top of me. At the moment of truth he withdrew and, looming over me, covered his cock and balls with his huge hands so I could not see them. The sheet below me was wet with my sweat and my fingers were between my legs. The clock on my bedside table said six a.m. I missed Beast and wished he was sitting on the bed staring at me, wanting to be fed. Sigh.

I managed to stagger up from the bed only to be hit in the head with the smell from last night's tuna fish and limburger cheese casserole. I needed to throw it out and the sooner the better. Suddenly I had a sense of purpose; I would take the trash down and put it in the garbage pails beside the front door and then come back up and clean my apartment. This is a reliable magic that has worked for me often before. I pulled on some jeans and a t-shirt, then went down the stairs carrying a full bag of garbage. I pushed open the front door.

A man was already there, going through the trash. He was wearing two wool caps, one red, one black, one on top of the other, a soiled beige parka and dark pants.

When I opened the door, he looked up and saw me. He pulled his mouth back in what was an enormous grin and then he licked his lips. His fly was open. He put in a grimy hand and pulled his glory out. It looked like a snake, long, glistening, oily. He shook it at me, vigorously up and down.

"Hey baby, baby, baby," he said. I threw the bag of garbage at him, then ran back inside, double locked the door, and dashed back upstairs to my apartment.

I have never actually flashed anyone, so I don't know what it feels like, but there seems to be certain exuberance, a gaiety to the gesture. My flasher this morning certainly looked happy. The first flasher I ever saw was my father and when he flashed me he was grinning. I must have been about four years old and my mother was giving me a bath. My grandmother called her out of the bathroom to take a phone call and then my father came in to pee.

"Hi ya, Duchess," he said, then he turned his back to me and stood over the commode. I heard the hissing sound of the steady stream hitting the water, he turned to face me again. "How's my daughter?" he said, with a grin as silly as Howdy Doody's grin on TV. He took his thing in both his hands and shook it at me slowly a few times, his fingers caressing it. Maybe he was not "consciously" exposing himself, ha, maybe he was just relaxed and not thinking about what he was doing, but he flashed me, no doubt about it.

Since then, besides the apparition this morning, I have seen flashers in the subway, on the streets of the city, in Prospect Park, Central Park, and once in the biography section of the Sheepshead Bay Public Library. I was ten and looking through a copy of Carl Sandberg's *Abraham Lincoln: The War Years*. My friend Lynn told me the best thing to do in such situations is to say, "Put that ugly little thing back in your pants. You should be ashamed of it." However, usually I would stare for an instant, transfixed, and then just turn tail and flee.

I used to see a lot more flashers around. Maybe the immoral "moral majority" and the fear of actual carnality, with its threat of STDs, have forced the flashers so far underground that they now work in tunnels beneath the subways.

I believe it is the same fear of carnality that keeps people from dancing at parties, a phenomenon that seems to be growing in the last few years. Maybe the real reason Clinton was elected to this second term was because he is a carnal guy and so many people who didn't have the courage to let it all hang out admire him.

I don't know. I do know that when I go out to parties in my newly single state and the music starts to play, usually no one gets up to dance except for Ursula and me. I have also noticed that if I am at a bar or an opening and a man is looking at me and I flash a smile back at him, he looks away. Maybe, this is a symptom of the current plagues of divorce, alienation, narcissism, nihilism or revisionism. Maybe he sees something in my smile that says I am a reformed masochist and he knows how dangerous that can be. Maybe he is trying to get up the courage to approach me. Maybe it is just not yet my lucky day, but I will do my best to keep smiling anyway.

Octopus' Garden

On August 31st, my birthday, twenty-five years ago today, a fisherman sat down beside me in the F 'ocsle, my favorite Provincetown dive. He said "I want you to be my mermaid tonight."He told me his name, Dickie Oldenquist. His eyes were the color of the ocean, his voice gentle. He smelled of salt and wind. I said yes.

We went to his house. Before we climbed into his bed he put Abbey Road on the record player in his bedroom and, during "Octopus' Garden," he entered me. We lived together for two years until when, on a fishing trip to the Outer Banks, his boat went down. Of the eight men on the Patricia Marie, he was the only one whose body was never found. Whenever I did something he didn't like or if he just wanted to get a rise out of me, he used to say, "Ah, the sea, the sea, the sea is the only woman who never betrayed me." When the harbor master showed up at our door to tell me Dickie was gone, my first thought was Oh, Dick, oh Dick.

It's summer now and my fifty-fourth birthday is next week. The ceiling fan in my apartment is broken and the air in the kitchen is so hot and sticky it weighs me down. I don't feel like moving. Every day I promise myself that tomorrow I will get out to the beach; then I spend the day aimlessly lying in bed watching soap operas and thinking about the mistakes I made in my life.

At least I'm excited about my new job, which starts in a few weeks. I will be teaching a course in how to write erotic fiction at the New School. I have written my syllabus and am working on lesson plans, but I waste too much time. I while away the day watching soap operas and in the evening, watching reruns of "Buffy, the Vampire Slayer" and drinking cheap red wine. I am drinking again, although at least not so much.

At night, my dead lovers float up through my drunken sleep to console me, especially Dickie O. He used to come though the door after a ten-day fishing trip yelling "Where are you? The big harpoon is home." We would down tabs of Sunshine acid from the jar under the bed and make love for days.

I wake up this morning, dreaming he is still inside me. I know I am lucky to have such magic memories, but I want new magic, new salt in my life. I want to weave a spell, to celebrate the future, to celebrate the new opportunities that I know will come my way, but I don't know where my mojo is. I seem to have lost it.

I get up out of bed and, on my way to the loo, see myself reflected in the mirror on the bathroom door. My eyes are red, my face is pale. My bleached-blonde hair hangs down to my shoulders in a sloppy, overgrown pageboy cut. Hair is a charm; I need a new hairdo, a new glamour.

My pal Tex, a rock and roll and blues singer just got a Rasta 'do, complete with extensions. Now she has platinum braids down to her waist and she looks like a Star Trek goddess. I can't afford such a ritzy style, but maybe I can get little braids or cornrows. I call Tex and she tells me she got her braids at Louise's African Hair Braiding in downtown Brooklyn on the corner of Willoughby and Jay Streets. I take the fifty dollars I have stowed away for the phone bill out of my underwear drawer and put it in the pocket of my jeans. I put on my Bob Marley T-shirt to show that even though I am white, I have soul.

I walk down Jay Street to Willoughby. I think about how alluring I will be with my new exotic hairdo. I find myself humming "Octopus' Garden," swaying to the beat as I walk. I pass a policeman who looks at me sharply, so I go back to walking at a sedate pace. I wouldn't want him to stop me for questioning.

I find Louise's African Hair Braiding. The salon is on the second floor above a lingerie store. The walls all the way up the stairs are pasted with photos of women with fantastic hairstyles. None of the women are white. As I reach the landing I hear a TV blaring loudly. I open the door and go in. There are four large African women seated around a little table. They are talking French. A huge television dominates one wall. One of the women has a turban of brightly colored African cloth wrapped around her head. She rises, takes a step towards me, "How can we help you?" she asks in English. I ask if she is Louise and she nods.

I tell her Tex had sent me. "Ah, la chanteuse," Louise says. She smiles. Her two top front teeth are gold and one of them has a ruby in it. "You want a hairstyle like your friend's?" she asks.

I tell her no, something simple, maybe cornrows straight back and I don't want any hair extensions. She asks for sixty dollars; I tell her I only have fifty. Louise says okay, even though one of the seated women says in French, *Elle ment* (she lies). I don't let on that I speak French.

Louise motions to the woman who said I was lying. When she rises from her chair I see she is enormously pregnant. Her belly sways before her like Jell-o. She beckons to a beauty chair. I sit down and she swivels the chair around so I am not facing the mirror. Maybe this is a mercy. Her face is closed and hard as she takes a pink bottle that says Luster's Cream Oil from the stand beside the chair and squeezes some on my head. She puts it down and picks up a big wire comb from the stand. She combs my hair straight and is not gentle about it. Then she starts to section off my hair, fixing each section with a little plastic clip.

I ask her name but she only grunts and says Taisez-vous (be quiet). I ignore that and introduce myself and then I lie and say I know I'm in good hands. I hate how I do this, I hate how, when someone rejects me, I get all Uriah Heep and try to ingratiate myself with them. Maybe Taisez-vous senses my self-hatred, maybe she uses it to punish me because she yanks my hair so tightly for the first braid that I cry out.

On the TV, "All My Children" has just started. Louise and the two other women are playing a game. Louise has a bunch of cowry shells in her hand. She throws them out on the table and leaves them there a minute as she and her companions gaze on them; then she gathers them up and throws them down again. I ask what the shells are for and Louise tells me they are for *les prognostic,* which I know is how you say "divination" in French. I decide to take this as a hopeful omen. I have come to the right place for a new look, a beginning for my new life.

Louise takes a cigarette from a pocket in her dress and reaches under the table to pull out a big scallop shell ashtray. I notice for the first time the walls are painted a blue-green turquoise like the color of the Mediterranean I swam in when I visited Sicily. Louise and the other hair stylists are wearing shell jewelry. Their African hairstyles look like the striations of shells, the long braids like sea grass. In my mind's eye I can see waves breaking on a sunny beach. I can feel Taisez-vous's belly behind me. Her breath comes in waves and I feel like I am drifting on a warm, gentle sea.

Suddenly "All My Children" is interrupted by a news bulletin. A man who resembles Walter Cronkite and looks very sad comes on the screen. He announces that outside a small town in Texas three white men have killed a black man. They dragged him behind their pick-up truck until his head separated from his body. It gets very, very still inside Louise's African Hair Braiding. The announcer's voice drones on with details of the horrible crime. The women at the table look pointedly away from me. Taisez-vous continues braiding my hair, only now it seems she is pulling it viciously tight; maybe she is trying to yank my head off my neck. She begins to mutter under her breath.

I am no longer floating on a gentle sea; I am falling down, down through turbulent waters, past the skeletons of ancient ships, past piles of chains and shackles. When I hit bottom, I am surrounded by sea ferns. Web-like branches loom everywhere above me. They trap me just as my own fears, fears of what I don't understand or can't control, so often trap me and pull me down into darkness.

I struggle to keep my eyes open underwater, but they fill with murky tears. I have no air left. I can't find my breath. I am about to faint, but then far above me, I see, glistening like a minute diamond, a faint speck of light. With all the strength I can muster, I start to kick up with my legs. My arms are so heavy I can barely lift them, but I push them above my head and force myself to go on. I feel Dickie's strong hands on my waist pushing me upward, up, up until I break though, cresting a wave and I'm floating forward into a bubble of light and then I am in Louise's braiding salon.

Sputtering, stuttering, I hear myself say in a trembling voice, "I'm sorry, so sorry. This is terrible, so bad. People who do things like that set us back a hundred years. I feel ashamed to be white." It is the truth.

There is a long silence, then Louise speaks up: "They are very, bad, bad men."

One of the other women says, "They got the ones that did it but that won't bring back the poor dead man." The tension in the air lessens. We look at each other, shaking our heads.

Taisez-vous pulls my head back against her belly. I hear the beating of her baby's heart. It sounds like the pulse you hear inside a shell. When she is finished, Taisez-vous turns my chair around so I face the mirror. My skin is pulled back taut over the bones of my face. Tiny cornrows are gathered into a tight coil at the back of my head. This makes my high cheekbones look even more prominent. My eyes look bigger and somehow my crooked nose appears straighter. I am different, changed. The face looking back at me is prettier, more graceful. "Tres belle, tres jolie," the women say. It is true. My head is elegant, neat. I am sleek as a sea otter and ready for anything.

About the Author

Tsaurah Litzky is a widely published writer of poetry, fiction, erotica, memoir, and commentary. Her publications include the poetry collections, *Baby On The Water,* (Long Shot Press) and *Cleaning The Duck* (Bowery Books) as well as fifteen chapbooks. Her most recent chapbook is a book of yoga poems, *Full Lotus* (NightBallet Press).

Her erotic writing has been included in numerous anthologies, among them the Best American Erotica series edited by Susie Bright, eight times. She wrote and directed a play about Bukowski, *Barfly Redux,* which had a successful run at FusionArts Museum in Manhattan.

Her writing has appeared in all of the Unbearables anthologies, most recently *From Somewhere To Nowhere: The End of the American Dream,* and in *The Careless Embrace of the Boneshaker* (great weather for MEDIA), *Sensitive Skin* and *New Verse News.*

Other publications include *The New York Times, The Outlaw Bible of American Poetry,* (Thunders Mouth Press), *Bowery Women Poems* (Bowery Books), *Jews: A Peoples History Of The Lower East Side,* Volumes 1&3, (Clayton Books), and *The Mom Egg Review.*

She has read and performed her writing in over eighty venues. In April 2017 in Prague she performed via Skype at the High Holy Mass of Poetry. Her work has been archived in the New York University Library in the Fales Collection.

She is also a collage artist. She is a member of the on-line poetry circle *Brevitas* and the Unbearables.

Tsaurah lives on the Brooklyn waterfront, where she can see the Statue of Liberty from her kitchen window.